DANIEL HARTJOY

PRESENTS

The
WEALTH BUILDER
Lifestyle

AN UNCOMMON GUIDE
ANYONE CAN USE
TO BUILD WEALTH AND LIVE
A RECESSION READY LIFE

How The Other 99% Can Get Rich

Methods For Mastery, Inc.

Methods For Mastery, Inc.
PO Box 904
Wauna, WA 98395

www.WealthBuilderLifestyle.com

This publication contains the opinions and ideas of the author. It is designed to provide competent and reliable information regarding the subject matter covered. The strategies in this book may not be suitable for every individual. Furthermore, it is sold with the understanding that neither the author nor the publisher are providing legal (financial or other) advice. If legal assistance is required, the services of a professional should be sought. The author and publisher specifically disclaim any liability that is incurred from the use or application of the contents of this book. No particular results are guaranteed or warranted by using the information contained within.

This book is a nonfictional work. Names and places have been changed to protect the privacy of all individuals. Any resulting resemblance to persons living or dead is entirely coincidental and unintentional. The events and situations are true.

Printed in the United States of America

First edition 2014

ISBN: 978-0-9905072-0-8

Dedicated to my beautiful and ever-supportive daughters, Courtney and Kaitlin

Contents

ACKNOWLEDGEMENTS

First, I want to thank all of my great mentors. Similarly, thanks goes out to the like-minded individuals that dedicate their lives to researching and improving the knowledge available to those of us who wish to better our lives.

Next, I would like to thank the readers. I'm so glad you found it within yourself to take action towards getting the most out of your life. For going above and beyond the norm, I truly wish you the best in life.

Special thanks goes out to all of my family and friends who really got behind me and supported me throughout this project. Without their love and support this book likely would have never come to be.

To my clients and the others who I have worked with: thanks for your faith in these ideas and for putting forth the effort to implement them in your lives.

INTRODUCTION

Welcome to The Wealth Builder Lifestyle! I'm glad you're here and I hope you'll spend a few minutes to read on a little further because what's ahead has the potential to dramatically change the outcome of your life. It can literally mean the difference between you retiring broke, or retiring a millionaire, regardless of your current income.

Now I know that sounds like the lead in to some get rich quick scheme but I assure you The Wealth Builder Lifestyle couldn't be further from that.

It's a sad fact that in a country with so much potential for prosperity, that at age 65 when most people hope to retire, the average net wealth is less than $200,000. That's not going to be nearly enough and it's not a position you want to find yourself in.

So what is "The Wealth Builder Lifestyle?" Whether we realize it or not, we all live a "Wealth Lifestyle." Through our daily habits and actions we are either building wealth, or we are destroying wealth, or maybe we are somewhere in between, or a combination of both, where we go through a cycle of positive wealth creation, followed by a cycle of wealth destruction. In the end, the result is an average net wealth of less than $200,000 at age 65.

So how do we ensure that you are not average with a net worth of less $200,000 and get you to the million dollar mark. We do this using proven wealth building strategies. Unfortunately, there is not one blanket wealth building strategy that works universally for everyone. This book will help you design a Wealth Builder Lifestyle that is personalized to your own individual strengths, weaknesses and personality.

The concepts in this book are not the typical strategies and methods that most wealth building books and systems focus on. You

3

are not going to be taught to flip real estate, invest in penny stocks, start a business or attempt any other get rich quick approach to building wealth. While most people are distracted by the lure of big money or getting rich effortlessly, they are overlooking the sure thing right in front of them.

Getting wealthy is not reliant on a large income or grand slam financial windfall. Anyone with an income has the potential to build wealth throughout their lifetime and retire rich. In this book you'll learn the uncommon approach that opens the doors to wealth for everyone. You don't need to change your life in an extreme way or take some high risk, high stress approach to successfully build wealth, but you do need to understand the mechanics and psychology of money.

90% of people handling money don't understand the mechanics of building wealth or don't have the psychological strength to follow through with the necessary actions. Here you'll learn the mechanics of wealth building that few know, but even more importantly you will learn how to control your wealth building (or destroying) psychology that determines your financial fate.

It's a lot easier than you would think, this program has been created to make it simple for you to determine your current financial situation, discover the methods that will work for you to quickly start building wealth, and clearly demonstrate the results you can expect to achieve when you follow your personalized plan.

The reason the rich keep getting richer and the poor keep getting poorer is not some big conspiracy, you are in full control of everything you need to become wealthy. The simple fact is, the rich live The Wealth Builder Lifestyle and the poor don't. If you struggle with understanding money and keep getting outmatched by the game, it's time for you to learn what it takes to start living a Wealth Builder Lifestyle.

How to Use the Program

It's very simple! Anyone can do it. With a little patience and persistence, you have the ability to complete it successfully and the reward will be well worth your effort!

I can say that with full confidence because this program was designed with one purpose in mind: to simplify the understanding of how wealth is created and destroyed and to give you a fool-proof strategy that you can use to consistently build wealth. It's not required to have a high income for this plan to work. Learning to live this lifestyle will make wealth building consistent and easy, in addition it will help you minimize the risk of financial loss.

This program is filled with tools and techniques to address various financial situations. Regardless of whether or not they all apply to you, don't feel like you have to fully understand and implement every last one of them to be successful. Even if you implement just a few new tactics, you can expect a dramatic change in your financial future. I'll warn you, some of the methods included go against popular thinking and even supposed financial experts' strategies. This program was not designed to be trendy or fit any particular dogma. There are lots of "financial experts" getting paid plenty to tell you what to do with your money, yet unfortunately the financial situation for too many is still getting worse.

We live in the information age, so if you go looking for information on personal finances you will find an overwhelming number of resources. Understandably, this leads to confusion and often a lack of action. Well, I've got some good news. You don't need an MBA to build wealth! So let's get started and you will be ready to start implementing new wealth building strategies by the end of the day. To make things go quicker, I would advise you to have a few things handy: a calculator, a current copy of all your bills and debts, a paycheck, and internet access if possible.

YOUR COMMITMENT

Nobody owes us anything. We all must take responsibility for our own financial well being.

Today, the average American has less than $3,800 in savings. Twenty five percent of Americans have *nothing* in savings. Most have no idea what their net worth is, how much debt they're in, or how much wealth they will need to maintain a decent standard of living when they retire. You will soon be able to answer all those questions with certainty and have a strategic plan to get you exactly where you want to be.

Retirement may be a long ways away, but how you **choose** to live today will determine how you **have** to live in those later years. Use the Wealth Builder Lifestyle method to ensure that you can live life to the fullest now and have certainty that you will retire in comfort. Later is not the time to take action. Being passive today can ultimately leave you helpless and at the mercy of others when you are the most vulnerable. Nobody should allow themselves to get boxed into that situation, especially since when that time comes you may not even be physically capable of changing your situation. You can easily avoid being put in that devastating scenario. The solutions are simple and achievable by anyone, you just have to decide to take the necessary steps.

The following program will walk you step-by-step through all the elements you need to transition into being a successful wealth builder. This approach will be within your financial means and abilities, so you can get started living the Wealth Builder Lifestyle immediately. By the time you finish this program you will have a detailed Wealth Builder Blueprint (a complete plan of action based on your specific situation, skills, desires, and abilities) that will create a clear path for you to start down the road to millionaire status.

This is easier than you probably believe. And surprisingly, it's available to almost anyone who is willing to apply the simple principles outlined within. The real reason the rich keep getting richer and the poor keep getting poorer is because the rich prosper off of the concepts outlined here, while the poor have either never been exposed to them or destroy their chances for success by accepting the belief that it won't work for them. Once someone says, "I can't," and accepts that statement as true, all hope is lost and they will never even try to turn the doorknob of the door standing between them and success. Even an unlocked door will remain an impenetrable barrier to someone who never even bothers to try turning the knob. The key to your financial success is right here: open the door and come inside!

When you are ready to commit to yourself—to make sure you can be secure, thrive, and prosper from today on through the end of your time—put it in ink and let's get started. It's real easy to just think or say something, but not as easy to actually do it. If you are ready to make a real decision and secure a great future for yourself, commit to it in writing as your pledge to follow through with consistent and focused action.

My Commitment

Name: _____

Write a compelling statement about why you will complete this course. State it in the positive and be sure to include the outcomes that are the most important to you to achieve!

I'm committed to completing this course because:

_____

_____

_____

_____

_____

_____

_____

_____

Date I Decided to Live a Rich Life and Die Wealthy:

Started on: _____/_____/_____

Date I Finished This Course and Fulfilled My Commitment:

Completed on: _____/_____/_____

Wealth is created by a lifestyle, not an income."
- Daniel Hartjoy

THE REALITIES OF WEALTH TODAY

A FEW POINTS TO CONSIDER

Have you ever asked yourself what separates the rich from the poor? The answer is simple: rich people understand and know how to manage money. I don't just mean they know how to earn, save, and spend it—they understand the psychology of money. You too will soon learn how to master the same skills they use which will allow you to continually build wealth through good times and bad.

Regardless of the amount of financial wealth you achieve in your life, you need more. No, not more money—more from life. Money can buy lots of things, but happiness is not one of them. It can, however, help you meet the needs required to live a life of true abundance, gratitude, and fulfillment.

Have you ever had to endure hard times or the pain of losing your home to the bank after working so hard for it? Have you ever been looked down on like someone that is less than adequate just because your car or lifestyle wasn't keeping pace with society's expectations?

If so, you may feel alone or possibly even like some sort of abnormal case. But let me assure you that couldn't be further from the truth. In these complex times many people are getting caught off guard without the financial education and resources to survive. No matter how you got here, you have arrived at the door that leads to never having to be in that position again.

You **can** have the life of your dreams filled with the cars, homes, vacations, and all the other great luxuries life has to offer. Whatever your motivation, you can do it. But it has to start right here, right now, with you.

Speaking of which, did you know that there have been many studies about what would happen if you took all the wealth from the rich and gave it to the poor? The amazing thing is that they all concluded the same thing: within a short timeframe, the rich would have all the money back. "How is that possible?" Well, the rich simply understand how money works. And what about those who don't? Let's just say that money doesn't stick around very long. With all the financial uncertainty in the world, the time for you to take control of your finances and look out for your own future could never be more right. So relax, and let's get started. I'm going to walk you through creating your own Wealth Builder Lifestyle, step-by-step.

It's Not Fair

The economic landscape always appears unfair and slanted in favor of those who are already rich. It is true that there are different rules at different levels of wealth and if you are not extremely wealthy, some won't apply to you. Fair or unfair, that doesn't mean you don't have the ability to successfully build wealth. The rules and economic climate will never be "fair" or "equal," so if you are waiting for the time when they are to build wealth, I'm sad to say, you will never build wealth.

The key to succeeding, regardless of your current level of wealth, is knowing the rules and strategies that apply to you. Then leverage that knowledge and start moving your way up the ladder. The fact that almost 80% of millionaires in the US are first generation rich should be encouraging. They learned what it takes to build wealth and did it, so can you.

GET THIS

If you go no further in this program, at least do yourself a favor and be sure you get this one critical point! What you focus on is what you get. For better or worse, that's how life works—regardless of what you want. If you're like me you've heard this a million times and know it well enough that you could easily repeat it, but that doesn't necessarily mean you get it. If your actions in life don't reflect that you understand how powerful this force is, you don't get it.

You may say, "Well, no—I take actions towards what I want even if I focus some of my attention on what I don't." Therein lies the rub. You can only cognitively control your focus while you are awake and consciously in charge. However, to think that is all the effort and focus you put in is naive and dangerous. In actuality, a large portion of the establishment of what something means to you and how it will influence your thoughts and actions is done subconsciously. Your subconscious mind will use **all** the inputs and information it has received from your conscious activities to establish your guiding principles. These principles affect your drive, mood, attitude, actions, and responses in everything you do.

So let me make becoming wealthy really easy for you. It's a one step process: just focus on it. Focus all of your conscious thoughts, mental inputs, and actions on becoming wealthy and you *will*. That may sound overly simple, but it's so true.

Your Conscious Focus

This is the intentional focus we put on something while we are awake and in control. When you are awake you get to steer the ship and direct what goes in to your mind. The things you focus on, have interest in, study, and surround yourself with are what will manifest in your life.

Your Inputs

You can't block out everything bad, nor live in a bubble. But you need to be a formidable gate keeper of what intel goes into your mind. There is a lot of stuff you don't want to consume in this world courtesy of the internet, cable television, games, and a million other sources of mind pollutants. You need to make a proactive effort to ensure that your mind is not getting filled with garbage that has no positive value to you. Worse yet, so much of what we consume daily can actually harm us and even kill any hope of fulfilling our dreams. So if you put in good, positive information, guess what? Your life will be positive and reflect what you put into it.

The reason this is so important is because your subconscious is at work non-stop. Your subconscious mind is on cruise control, using this information to come up with the intelligence (or lack thereof) that runs your life. If you want to be successful and have a great life then read, watch, and proactively pursue sources of information on those topics. You want financial success? Get some related magazine subscriptions, surround yourself with successful people, and attend courses or seminars on the topic.

Your Subconscious Powerhouse

We focus the majority of our attention on our conscious thoughts and experiences with no regard for the most powerful and influential part of our mind. Have you ever pondered an idea or got hung up trying to find a particular solution only to one day have a seemingly arbitrary epiphany? That didn't just arrive from nowhere.

A breakthrough often occurs when your subconscious mind gets the last piece of the puzzle. Then it can finally provide your conscious self with the answer you've been asking for. That solution came from your subconscious processing all of the information you have consumed to date. When you take in an abundance of new and relevant information on what you seek, your mind can return better answers much more quickly.

Ever had déjà vu? The Merriam-Webster dictionary defines it as 'the illusion of remembering scenes and events when experienced for the first time'. To examine what's really going on here, let's back up a bit. So you are inputting all this information into your mind and your subconscious, right? And unbeknownst to you it is continually processing that data and trying to decide what these facts mean to you. To evaluate those things, your intellect must subliminally run through different what-if scenarios and try to determine what the likely outcome would be in addition to what effect it would have on you. So when you have déjà vu, I believe it's because things have played out in one of the ways your subconscious has already considered.

To the best of my knowledge, the belief I just shared is not backed up by science. That being said, I believe in this concept because it keeps me aware that whatever I expose myself to is being further processed by my subconscious. The subconscious mind steers our lives by building habits that influence our default actions based on the information it has previously received. These automatic responses will dictate our lives unless overridden by conscious choice and willpower—and we all know how well that typically works out. Therefore, we need to be damn sure we limit the information we receive to only the most beneficial type: the kind that will naturally lead us to making advantageous decisions that will ultimately lead to the life of our dreams.

The Take Away

To be a successful wealth builder you need to consciously, consistently, and proactively feed your mind information of only the most relevant and supportive types: the kinds that will lead you to naturally making superior decisions. You may say, "Ugh, I don't want to learn all this stuff!" I get that. But if you don't, you will struggle financially for a lifetime and *that* is ultimately much harder than figuring out wealth building.

Remember this key element. Most of the real learning and understanding of all the information you need to successfully build wealth happens subconsciously without any effort from you. So luckily, you don't have the full burden of trying to figure all of this out consciously.

I'm not trying to get you to subscribe to some crazy philosophy (although if crazy stands out and will help you remember it, great). I just want you to be aware that far more is happening behind the scenes in your mind than you may realize. So just proactively filter out the stuff you don't want more of in your life and feed your mind information and experiences that support you getting what you actually want.

It's truly that simple. If you do that, your tree will bear all the fruit you can stand.

NOTES :

_____

_____

_____

_____

_____

_____

_____

FOUR KEYS TO BEING RICH

There are four keys that you must master to become and stay rich. All four are critical, and coming up short on just one can be the difference between making it and getting caught in a death spiral towards being emotionally and financially broke. When you look at this list it may appear overly straightforward, like everything you have ever heard and continue to hear about. But don't cheat yourself with the assumption that you have already heard all of this before and completely understand it.

Behind each one of these benign-looking keys are a million different philosophies and strategies. What you will learn from this book is the Wealth Builder Lifestyle philosophy, which was created to make wealth building so simple and bulletproof that anyone can do it. By the end of this program you will fully understand how to use all of these keys without having to think about them. You will design a powerful Wealth Building Lifestyle that will be based on habitually creating wealth without the need for complex or cumbersome financial strategies.

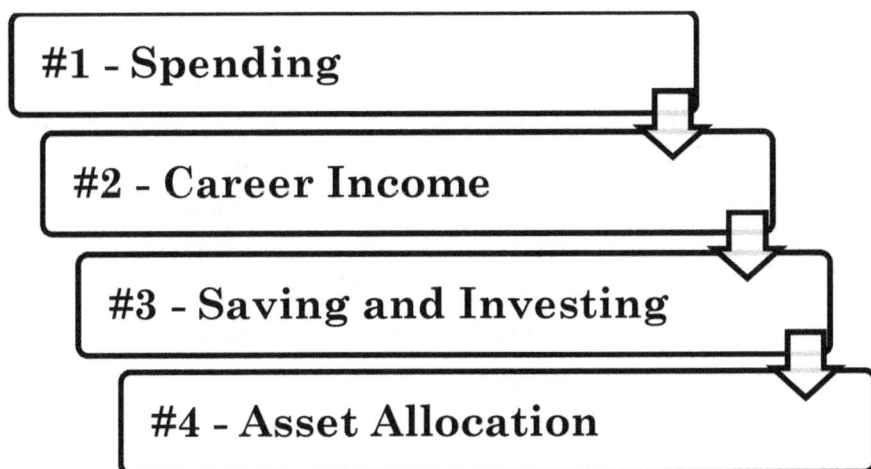

#1 - Spending

#2 - Career Income

#3 - Saving and Investing

#4 - Asset Allocation

Spending

This is number one because regardless of how much you earn you can always outspend your income. How many people have you seen increase their income and then their spending right along with it? You could be earning $15,000 a month and still be living paycheck to paycheck. Believe me, I know plenty of people that are in that exact situation—not building wealth and on the brink of financial collapse.

It may seem obvious that you need to spend less than you earn, but many don't. There is an extreme amount of social pressure to have and do so many things that you can easily spend any amount of money. Luckily, there is a wealth builder formula for spending that I will show you. This is the easy part, because it's simply a matter of mathematics.

On the other side of that coin (and the number one reason most people can't control their spending) is the emotional component. When it comes to spending, emotion is far more influential on our habits than our intellectual understanding of money. I'll also be showing you how to take control of your emotions so that you have a fighting chance to break our current societal trend of ever-increasing financial insecurity and poverty.

Career Income

Your career income is the fastest way for you to create wealth in your earlier years. The expectation is that when you are young your pay will be low and you will have to use most or all of it just to get by. Then as your skills and experience increase, you will be able to afford to live a better life and finally have the disposable income to start investing. That is a huge mistake. As logical as that might sound, it is absolutely foolish and a part of the mentality that keeps people poor.

A wealth builder needs to focus in on fast-tracking their careers early. Career fast-tracking is one of the largest topics covered in this program, and for good reason. The sooner we can get your career income up—even if only by a small percentage—the faster your wealth creation will grow and new doors of opportunity will open.

The economy we are currently living in will not allow you to prosper using the strategies of the past. I'm not trying to be a downer by talking about the fact that our economy is in shambles and struggling right now. This is a temporary problem for our society that has actually opened up an abundance of opportunities for people like you and me. If you aren't already seeing them, you definitely need to commit to finishing this program. I will not only show you how to fast-track your career in *any* economy, but I'm also going to talk in depth about what's ahead and how you can prosper while others struggle to find their way.

The new economy that's going to emerge after the smoke clears from the current recession will look like nothing we have ever seen before. There will be an abundance of people trapped in poverty, a growing class of the super wealthy, and a smaller middle class made up of visionary business owners and employees using the latest cutting-edge strategies of tomorrow.

I created this system to make sure you have a chance to be in one of the latter two. There will be plenty of room at the bottom for all those who don't respond to these changes and rise to the challenges currently taking place. The fact that you picked up this program tells me that you are someone who is putting forth the effort to get informed and take action to make their life better... And *that* gives you a distinct advantage over the average person.

Saving and Investing

Most people look at these as two separate categories, but I look at them as one since you can't invest if you don't save. Saving—to me—is just a part of investing. Anything you save is an investment in securing your future, regardless of whether it is earning a return or not. You will be establishing a personalized saving and investing plan based specifically on your income and financial situation. It will be designed with the sole intent of catapulting you into the strongest possible wealth building scenario.

Your investment income will eventually subsidize or replace your career income as your career income fades or ends all together. Our goal will be to help you establish consistent habits of doable investment contributions throughout your working years. This way, by the time you need it your investment income will be in its prime life cycle. Life cycles, by the way, are an amazing force that continually affect every facet of your life. I will demonstrate how they are a key element in any successful wealth building strategy so you can incorporate them into your blueprint for becoming a millionaire.

Asset Allocation

Last but not least by any means is asset allocation. Regardless of how much wealth you have built it needs to be kept safe from any one market fluctuation. Ask all those people that lost their homes during the "housing crisis" how important asset allocation is. So many people had all their past wealth and current income going into their home only to have it swept out from under their feet due to a market shift. Unfortunately, since they weren't properly prepared, there was little they could do to prevent it.

I admire those who are willing to dedicate and commit to something 100% like those who went all-out to get a home. I don't, however, admire the situation they put themselves in by having all their eggs in one basket. In that regard, they learned a vital lesson about asset allocation the hard way.

You might be asking, "What could they have done?" Some lost their jobs, and others had bad loans. Well, it surely would have helped if they had made sure to fully fund a security cushion prior to buying that home. Or perhaps if they had some other investments or assets then they would have had more options. The majority of those who lost their homes lost them because they couldn't truly afford them in the first place. Unfortunately, they were relying solely on their career income cash flow when making their decision.

The Wealth Builder Lifestyle has boundaries designed to help you avoid making purchases you can't afford, getting overleveraged by debt, and protecting you from individual market fluctuations. You will determine and setup those specific boundaries to protect your future wealth.

Being Rich Is Not Being Wealthy

"What?" You may say. I'm here to help, so I have to keep it real. No amount of money will ever lead to lasting happiness. Let's face it: you don't want to be rich so you can have a bunch of pieces of paper with dead presidents on them. I know plenty of people that are definitively rich but no happier than some of my poor acquaintances—maybe even less so.

If you are following this program solely with the intent of getting financially rich, you may find the money more of a curse than a blessing. Unless you understand what it really takes to have a fulfilling life, money will only help you live a similar life to what you currently have in a more opulent style. Make no mistake, if your heart and intentions are in pursuit of money for the wrong reasons, you can expect lots of pain to accompany your success.

Which brings me to my next point. There may be four keys to being rich, but there is...

NOTES :

_____

_____

_____

ONLY ONE WAY TO BE WEALTHY

If you truly want to be wealthy in your life, you need to look outside of money and into successfully living a fulfilling life. This is an extensive topic on its own so there is no way it's going to fit in this book, but I do want to share the broad concept with you. If you will keep these seven human needs in mind as you go through this course and life in general, all aspects of your life will make more sense and you will have much greater control over your happiness.

The Seven Human Needs

The human needs aspect of this program is designed to help you understand what motivates all humans. This includes what is necessary to keep ourselves in balance and ultimately, deliver inner peace. These needs are not something we can just put off meeting—they *have* to be successfully met to live any kind of meaningful life. A great life can never be achieved without substantially meeting most or all of these needs. Understanding these needs and keeping them well served in all aspects of your life will give you the opportunity to live a truly enjoyable and fulfilling life.

The needs below are listed in the order of significance in our lives. This does not mean that we all value and work to meet these needs in this particular order.

Sustenance

This is the essential need we all must meet to even *exist*. We meet this requirement with things like food, water, shelter, money, and other items we would perish without. If these essentials are ever endangered, our survival instincts kick in and give us the ability to conquer obstacles we previously thought were impossible.

Connection

Connection is the most powerful and influential need we all have, and often one of the most underserved and overlooked. Without question, this is an area you want to focus a lot of attention on. We often evaluate our connections by who we know that we can use to make things happen. That is a very basic way of looking at connections, but it does actually do a good job of illustrating the power and importance of having good ones.

If you are ever in a pinch and need someone to lean on or help you find an opportunity, the most reliable source for a solution is in your connections. Even a loose connection can often provide some wisdom or make you aware of an opportunity that can resolve your problem. In my life I have been blessed with some good connections long before I ever understood their value.

Our need for connection must be met from many meaningful sources including family, friends, strangers, coworkers, pets, the environment, and society in general. When you have the capability to make significant connections on a deeper level (and just as importantly, fulfill the connection need for others), an entire new world of opportunity and security will open up to you.

Security

Frequently the most focused on need, security, gives us the certainty that we can do things like take care of our family. We will often forgo our connection need to instead dedicate our focus and energy towards meeting our security need. This makes sense at first glance, but in reality the easiest way to meet and achieve security is to have and maintain solid connections.

Growth

To live a fulfilling life you *need* to constantly be growing. There are no plateaus that allow for you to remain in one spot. Life is constantly in motion, moving in one direction or another, and by choosing to grow you avoid contracting. Growing your education, finances, experiences, and so on keeps life interesting and provides a feeling of truly being alive.

This doesn't need to be a large burden. Reading something that will increase your knowledge for even just 15 to 30 minutes a day can keep you growing intellectually. Living a Wealth Builder Lifestyle will constantly be growing your net worth, as well.

Significance

We all need to feel significant, like we matter. This feeling adds meaning to our lives, builds us up, and makes us feel important. Often times this need is very ego driven: why do we want to build an empire, have fancy cars, and own nice things? It's because in today's society those things are symbols of success—meaning you have achieved something beyond average—and are therefore special.

We need to be very careful when serving this need because it is too easily met in unhealthy, immoral, or selfish ways. Those negative approaches defy our inner human values and will never provide anything other than short-term results.

This is where buyer's remorse comes from. We may buy something that makes us feel cool, at least momentarily. But soon after, the coolness wears off and we realize it didn't make us special. Now we have maxed-out credit cards we will have to make payments on for the next few years for something we didn't ultimately want or need. This leads to us feeling foolish and, depending on our financial position, may actually negatively impact our need for security (which compounds our bad feelings).

There are far cheaper, more fulfilling, and longer lasting ways to meet our need for significance. One healthy option is through contribution, which doesn't need to involve money at all. In fact, dedicating some of your time to better your community by mentoring someone in need can be far more fulfilling than you'd expect.

THE REALITIES OF WEALTH TODAY

Just the other day I decided I would try something new and use public transportation for the adventure. I rode a bus to a BART train (part of a rapid transit rail system), rode that to San Francisco, walked 1.5 miles through downtown and along Fisherman's Wharf, and finally caught a ferry from there to Sausalito. I got an impromptu drive-by tour of Alcatraz Island Prison and met some nice tourists. I was able to be of service and share some local knowledge with these visitors about their destination.

Not only did this turn out to be a great experience but it also helped me meet a lot of my needs: I formed connections with some great people and got more in touch with the community; I grew by learning how to get around without my car; and I increased my sense of personal significance by sharing local knowledge with some interested tourists.

Esteem

When this need is fulfilled, it's often because we are achieving things. We have the respect of others, feel confident, are proud, and are experiencing increased drive. Esteem is not to be mistaken for just self-esteem, they are both equally important. Our need is met in two ways: internally, through self-esteem (how we truly think and feel about ourselves), and externally, through esteem (which is how we are regarded and seen by others).

As anyone knows, having self-esteem is a very important aspect of being successful. Less focused on in today's "me" society, however, is the power of regular esteem. Today, we are more likely to bully or buy our way through or around obstacles. This may work out in the short-term, but it's not a lasting approach.

So, how do you successfully meet your need for esteem? The best way is to adequately meet the previously mentioned needs. There is absolutely no reason why you wouldn't be held in high esteem and feel high self-worth (which leads to self-esteem) if you: can easily **sustain** yourself; have great **connections** with your friends, family, boss, environment, and community; are financially and personally **secure**; are continually **growing** your knowledge, wealth, connections, and emotional intelligence; and are feeling **significant** because you are continually contributing to your family, friends, and society in general.

Inner Peace

Inner peace is what compels us to continually pursue all of our other needs. Should we fail to successfully fulfill them in healthy ways that align with our values, we will feel pain. The further away we are from satisfying our needs, the more pain and despair we can expect.

The key to meeting this seventh need is first focusing on meeting the other six. Once you have mastered that, you will have energy, passion, and drive like never before. This will bring you to the final step, which is acceptance. When you accept your life and its purpose you can then feel at peace and ultimately fulfilled. Unchecked, our quest for inner peace will either drive us to success (if we're lucky) or insanity (if careless). Nonetheless, we will continue our pursuit until we achieve it or reach our end. This may all seem like psycho babble, but I assure you it's not. It's undeniable that every human has the need to meet these seven elements. Take a look at anyone who is truly successful financially, career-wise, in relationships, in regard to life balance, in parenting, and in all the other aspects of their lives. You will find that they will all have these two things in common:

1. They will be substantially meeting most (if not all) of their needs.
2. They will be very influential in helping others meet their own needs.

That being said, few successful people would actually be able to tell you about their human needs or how they meet them. They don't need to because they have picked up habits that effectively meet their needs throughout their upbringing and life experiences. In a way, you could say they're just lucky. But success does not require you to be lucky. Once exposed to and made aware of these needs, anyone can reshape the environments and habits of their life to adequately meet them. The beauty is that when you are meeting your needs, you will realize just how little money it actually takes to live a rich and fulfilling life.

Balancing Self and Public Image

When it comes to image, early wealth builders have to be very honest with themselves. One of the most powerful forces that can work against wealth building (especially in the U.S.) is maintaining an image of wealth. The reason why said image can get the better of so many is due to the fact that it artificially meets some of the seven human needs. This is no joke. This *will* be an Achilles heel for many aspiring wealth builders. You may have to do some serious re-training to detach yourself and stop spending money to artificially meet your needs.

Many things we buy can give us a feeling of self worth or esteem. I'm not saying it's all bad. On the contrary, I believe there are times when it's absolutely necessary to spend money to support your image. Unfortunately, if you are putting off wealth building and spending money to support an image you can't afford, some day you will be delivered a harsh and unforgiving reality. Below are some brief examples of how spending can meet some needs and support your image unnaturally.

Sustenance

Having income or cash flow can easily satisfy this need, especially if you are not consciously aware of your overall financial picture and risk. Being a little low on money may not trigger concern when another paycheck is expected soon.

Connection

By using money, you can be the life of the party. Thanks to your artificially rich image, you can have an abundance of social interactions and a long list of people waiting to hang out with you. With all those connections and great times, your friends and family will rally around you and worship you like a god—at least until the money is gone.

Security

Once again, without a clear understanding of your finances and the world of money, you can foolishly believe you are secure just because you have another paycheck due in the near future. As naïve as that is, this can falsely appear to meet your security need.

Growth

Taking trips, seeing places, figuring out how to operate the new smart TV, growing your credit lines, meeting new people, and so on are all sources of growth that will meet this need right up until you run out of money. This may project an image of having a great life while in reality you're living on the edge.

Significance

Spending is the number one socially accepted method for attempting to artificially meet our need for significance. Drive a fancy car, wear fancy clothes, or own all the latest gadgets and toys and you will feel and look very significant indeed. If you want to test how wise of a game this is, just compare your stuff to the truly wealthy. Oh yeah, that sucks! Worse yet, theirs is likely paid for in full and actually *theirs*.

Esteem

When you have an abundance of friends and your needs are met (even artificially), you are going to feel pretty good about yourself and how you are viewed by others. Just don't let that party stop.

Inner Peace

You may have moments of bliss, but if you have any kind of financial intelligence—even just a little bit—you are going to have some concern about the what-ifs. What if my income stops? How long can I sustain myself if that happens? Questions like these won't have good long-term answers. Unfortunately, many will just accept their needs being artificially met and continue enjoying the moments of bliss in the present without any regard for the future fallout.

You do not want your worth tied to money that someday you may not be able to obtain or that you find may be in limited supply. When people that live that way suffer from financial setbacks, a huge void forms on their "needs being met" list and they feel distraught. Others have even taken their own lives just to get out of the pain of feeling so empty and broken. That is not a game that's worth playing, especially when there are better options that are sustainable throughout time.

So what's a good boundary for new wealth builders? Well, that varies from person to person, but if success in your career requires you to maintain a certain image you will certainly need do what you have to do... Just do it honestly. Don't use your career as the justification for you to go out and buy every piece of trendy clothing, make a foolish car purchase, or try to always have the latest and greatest. Very few careers (if any) require that type of financial foolishness.

There also has to be some balance to accommodate your self-worth (and consequently, your self-esteem). If your car is such a jalopy that your children are getting ridiculed by their peers in school, saving those dollars may have too high of an emotional cost to make it worthwhile. Once again, this is not a license to jump right back in to the game of keeping up with the Joneses. Get yourself a cost-effective vehicle that doesn't humiliate you and your family. Trust me, the humility will pay off when it's time to compare financial statements.

Four States of Living

Something to consider in wealth building (and life in general) includes the four states of living. Regardless of the amount of wealth you have or want, you need to be conscious of the state you are living in. Make sure the state you are spending most of your time in is serving the ultimate goal of living a fulfilling life. We can often greatly accelerate our lives' forward progress by being aware of and choosing which state we are living in.

Intentionally sacrificing for a period of time can greatly accelerate growth, which may (for some) be the shortest path to a life of fulfillment. That being said, we need to make every effort to ensure that we do not get stuck in a lifestyle of sacrificing and/or sustaining. This happens all too often since these take the least amount of effort and require very little proactive action to attain.

There's a good chance that you'll have to sacrifice for a while as you transition into a lifestyle of wealth building. However, your wealth builder plan takes this into consideration and if sacrificing is necessary, you will have an exit strategy to get out of that state within twelve months.

This period of sacrificing is often a requirement to break out of a life of just sustaining, which the majority of people are currently stuck in. Sustaining is not a great place to live. It is painful enough that most will complain and grouse, but it's not so bad that those whining will actually do anything about it.

With the majority of people living a lifestyle of just sustaining themselves, it's really easy to find social proof that confirms you are average. You could, facing this evidence, let yourself off the hook rather than change. But before you do, consider this: the average person does not necessarily live a great life and will likely retire in poverty.

You, however, don't *have* to be average. This program holds all the tools and knowledge you need to move from an ordinary life into an extraordinary one.

This graphic illustrates the states we ideally want to spend the most time living our lives in.

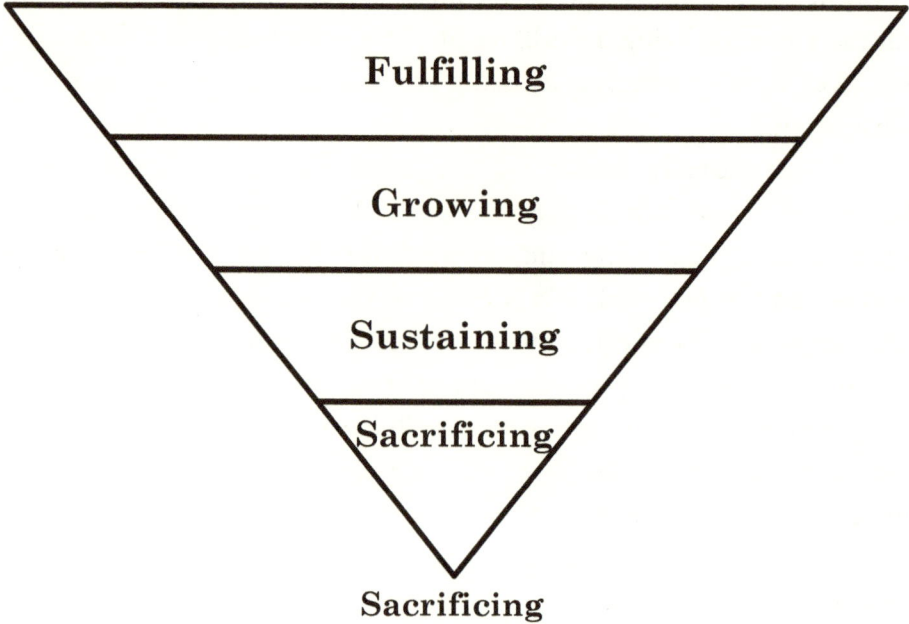

```
         Fulfilling

          Growing

         Sustaining

        Sacrificing
```

Sacrificing

Sacrificing is not a state we want to live our lives in forever. On the other hand, short stays with the intent of leveraging an opportunity that has long-term benefits which can propel us up into a better state of living can often make sense. But ultimately, a fulfilling life will be one that spends very little time in this state of living.

Sustaining

This can be one of the most limiting and dangerous states of living. Often times when people are able to sustain themselves, they tend to fall into the old cliché of "this is making a living." Sustaining is a high-risk state of living. Without intention or awareness of the importance of building real wealth, this can become a trap that can lead to spending the last years of your life in a forced state of sacrificing.

Growing

Often growing can be one of the most fulfilling states of living, but it typically requires clear goals and decisive intentions to enter into and maintain this state. A lifestyle involving growth will open doors to many of life's greatest opportunities such as an abundance of wealth, social success, new knowledge, interpersonal triumphs, relationship victories, and other areas of great importance.

Fulfillment

A life in balance (filled with growth and the rewards of achievement in many areas of life) can lead to the greatest state of living, and ultimately, a life of fulfillment.

NOTES :

_____

_____

_____

_____

_____

_____

_____

_____

_____

_____

LIFE CYCLES
AFFECT AND INFLUENCE
EVERYTHING

Life cycles are essentially the changing states that everything goes through. Depending on the life cycle stage something is in, it will often return different results or responses. Some of these life cycles are well known and focused on, especially in business. Not taking these into consideration in business can lead to large profit losses or worse— going out of business.

These life cycles are also present in our daily lives. They affect our income potential, household expenses, transportation costs, personal expenditures, education, and on and on. Although life cycles affect everyone, it depends on the individual's situation when and how they will show effect.

As you will see in the following examples, putting off investing until your income is substantial enough to contribute larger amounts is foolish. Even small amounts invested early on will turn into large sums by the time you retire. Don't underestimate the power of compound interest. Use it wisely to turn pennies into dollars. For example, $1 invested at 10% when you are 20 will be worth $88 when you're 65. If you wait until you're 40 to start investing, you will have to invest $7.50 to get to that same $88 by age 65. So $20 invested at 20 is just as powerful as $150 invested at 40. It is never a bad thing to start investing early, but it is certainly detrimental to wait too long.

Career Income Life Cycle

A good example of an important life cycle involves our income-earning potential.

Stage One encompasses ages 18-25 when we have few skills, low income, and less stability.

Stage Two encompasses ages 25-35 when we have high skill development, increasing income, and more stability.

Stage Three encompasses ages 35-50 when we are in our peak-earning years. We are masters of our skills, have the highest income-earning potential, and are very stable.

Stage Four encompasses ages 50-65, which I call the twilight years of earning. We are coming off of our peak: our skills are fading, our income has likely stagnated (or may be decreasing), and our job stability is in question. Losing a job at this stage in life can mean a huge pay reduction and possibly even permanent unemployment.

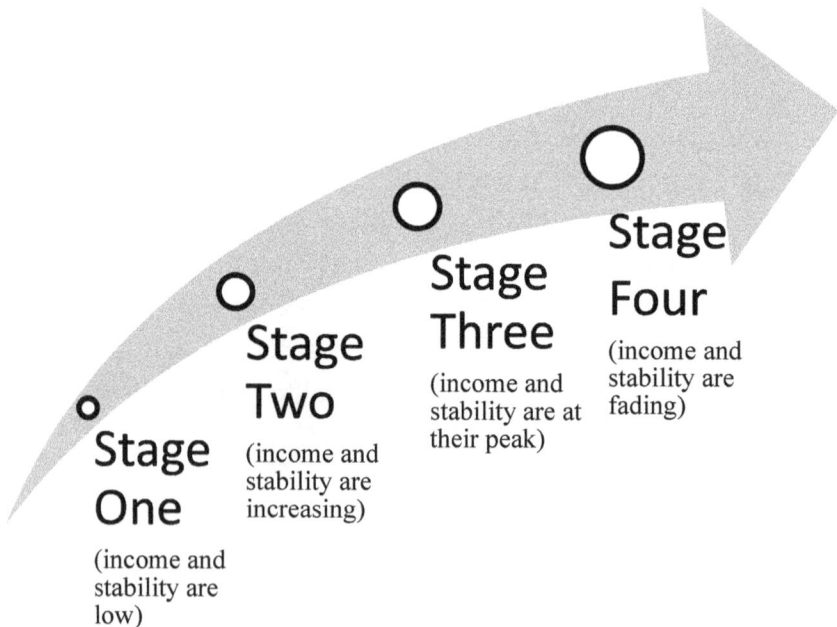

Stage One
(income and stability are low)

Stage Two
(income and stability are increasing)

Stage Three
(income and stability are at their peak)

Stage Four
(income and stability are fading)

LIFE CYCLES AFFECT AND INFLUENCE EVERYTHING

Investment Income Life Cycle

Now, with the career income life cycle in mind, look at the investment income life cycle and see how they can work with or against each other. The most powerful time to invest is when your income is in Stage One because even a small investment at this point will be exploding in value during Stage Four of your career income-earning cycle (which, if you'll recall, is when stability and income potential are falling). A lifetime of good investing habits can lead to eventually replacing your lost career income with investment income. Unfortunately, most will wait until they have an abundance of extra money to start investing, resulting in their investments not having the necessary time to reach their own peak growth cycles.

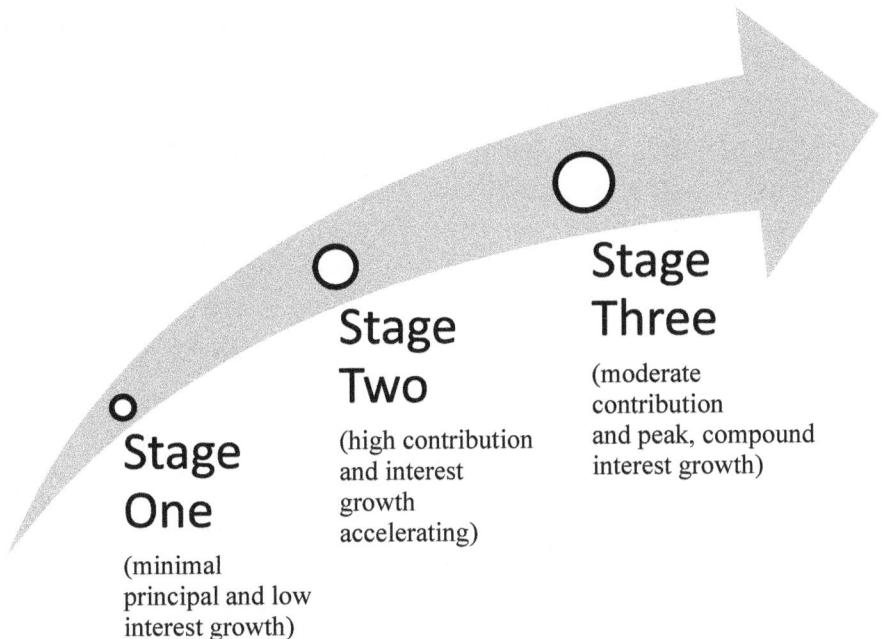

Stage Three

(moderate contribution and peak, compound interest growth)

Stage Two

(high contribution and interest growth accelerating)

Stage One

(minimal principal and low interest growth)

THE REALITIES OF WEALTH TODAY

For you to successfully control and leverage lifecycles to their fullest benefit requires a broad analysis. At first, that may sound contradictory considering many wealth building tools are focused on individually. But the difference when considering life cycles is that to successfully capitalize on them you often times have to work the yin against the yang (and vice versa). So a narrow focus on one problem (the yin, or the career income in this case) may keep you from seeing the natural solution that comes from the yang (the future investment income).

When it comes to wealth building, career and investment incomes should be viewed as one interconnected tool. Too many people get focused on one and let the other lay dormant. The optimal way to build wealth is through a balanced two-prong approach. When you retire and your paycheck stops, your investments will continue to produce income through the end of your days. Remember, maximizing your income-growth potential early will allow you to rapidly increase your investments, which will greatly accelerate the effects of compound interest and multiplicatively explode your lifetime wealth-creation potential.

NOTES :

_____

_____

_____

_____

_____

_____

_____

_____

THE VALUE OF A DOLLAR

We hear about the dollar losing value all the time these days. For some this may be the case, but for the people living the Wealth Builder Lifestyle it's actually far from it. The rich know that to not lose their wealth to inflation they need to keep their money invested and working hard (as opposed to just trying to save it). By having their money invested into an investment that is earning a compound return that *exceeds* the rate of inflation, their dollars are not losing but instead *gaining* value. Perhaps that is in part why Albert Einstein is quoted as saying, "It is the greatest mathematical discovery of all time," when referring to the effects of compound interest.

The next time you spend a dollar on something you could do without, consider what that dollar would be worth if you stashed it away in an investment instead. The following chart illustrates just that—the explosive returns you could expect from compound interest. Teaching your kids to put away even small amounts of money when they are young will allow them to easily build wealth throughout their own lifetime (and retire with financial security).

The saying "time is money" is absolutely true when it comes to investing. A $1 investment with a 10% return will grow to $7.32 in 20 years. That's not bad, seeing as that's over seven times its original value. But let it compound *another* 20 years and it will be worth a whopping $53.70! That's over 53 times the value. Wow! That Einstein fella might have been onto something.

This chart shows what an investment of just $1 (one time) would be worth over different periods of time based on varying rates of return.

"Take strategic actions to create exceptional results with minimal effort!"

- Daniel Hartjoy

Value Over Time of $1 Investment (Excluding tax consequences)						
Return	1 Year	5 Years	10 Years	20 Years	30 Years	40 Years
3.0%	$1.03	$1.16	$1.34	$1.82	$2.45	$3.31
5.0%	$1.05	$1.28	$1.64	$2.71	$4.46	$7.35
7.5%	$1.07	$1.45	$2.11	$4.46	$9.42	$19.89
10.0%	$1.10	$1.64	$2.70	$7.32	$19.83	$53.70
12.5%	$1.13	$1.86	$3.46	$12.02	$41.70	$144.62
15.0%	$1.16	$2.10	$4.44	$19.71	$87.54	$388.70
17.5%	$1.18	$2.38	$5.68	$32.28	$183.47	$1,042.57
20.0%	$1.21	$2.69	$7.26	$62.84	$383.96	$2,790.74
22.5%	$1.24	$3.04	$9.29	$86.34	$802.31	$7,455.18
25.0%	$1.28	$3.44	$11.87	$140.98	$1,673.95	$19,875.79

This also illustrates the harsh reality of waiting to start investing. The peak return on long-term, compound interest investments comes in the later years, so the longer it has to work the more it can do. This is one reason there is great value in setting up investments for your children or grandchildren at birth. Such a strategy will give that investment over sixty years to grow! It just goes to show that even a minimal amount (set aside early) can have a huge impact on how well your children are setup for their own retirement. The same goes for college tuition: the sooner you start investing, the better.

Consider this: to be a millionaire after 40 years, you only need to invest $18,621 one time into a 10% return investment. And if you could pull off a 15% return, that amount drops to just $2,572.

Debt Reduction Investing

If you want to swing quickly from financial fool to fast-track wealth builder, here is one way to do it.

Say you're just getting started, but are amped up and ready to take a small step. You have decided that you can immediately put $50 a month into your new Wealth Builder Lifestyle. If you have any short-term debt, one of the best investments you can make is getting yourself out of it.

Let's keep it real here: credit cards are the bankers' wealth building tools. But for a consumer, a credit card is a poor way of faking wealth. Worse yet, they can hold people back from ever actually becoming wealthy! If you have credit cards or some other form of short-term debt, don't tell me you're not broke. If you're not, then why are you spending someone else's money? Even worse, you're paying them a high interest rate just for using it!

I'm going to assume for this example that you have some credit card debt (as the majority of people do). Let's say you owe $5,000 worth, and let's also assume the interest rate on that debt is 18%. Now, I'm sure *you* don't have that debt, but maybe a friend does so stay tuned. Maybe this bit of insight could be shared and do them some good.

I'm going to illustrate this in a few different ways so you can understand the deeper dynamics in play. These are all things that banks and wealthy people know and habitually avoid. One of the keys to this wealth building system is to get you into good habits and away from the bad ones. Regardless of whether you fully understand the reasoning, this will help you minimize wealth loss and be more likely to create it.

First, let's look at your debt based on the previously outlined criteria. Assuming you will pay it off using the minimum payment (calculated by the lender at 2% of the balance), here are the numbers:

Typical Payoff

Initial Debt: **$5,000**
Initial Payment: **$100**
Total Interest Paid (wealth squandered): **$11,898**
Time to Pay Off: **32 years and 10 months**

THE REALITIES OF WEALTH TODAY

Look at the dramatic difference below that would result if you made just one extra payment of $50 towards this card (and then paid it off using the minimum payment schedule):

One $50 Extra Payment
(then typical payoff)

Initial Debt: **$5,000**
Initial Payment: **$100**
One-Time Payment: **$50**
Total Interest Paid (wealth squandered): **$11,348**
Time to Pay Off: **31 years and 8 months**

That $50 actually saves you $500 over the life of the loan and shortens the loan by 1 year and 2 months!

Now, let's say you lock yourself into a new, self-imposed minimum payment of $150 (which is essentially your current minimum payment plus a $50 investment). This is what it would look like doing some debt investing in yourself:

Fixed Payment Debt Investing

Initial Debt: **$5,000**
New Debt-Investment Payment: **$150**
Total Interest Paid (wealth squandered): **$1,835**
Time to Pay Off: **3 years and 10 months**

That debt-investment wealth building strategy will save you a whopping $10,063 in less than four years! If you don't have that extra money already, then you really need to ask yourself how you can afford to give away over $10,000 to a bank. I'm sure you appreciated them lending you that $5,000 so you could buy a few feel-good things, but that time has long passed and now you're saddled with years of feel-*bad* credit card payments.

THE VALUE OF A DOLLAR

Before we go any further, here's a tip: **never just pay the minimum payment!** Never, never, never. So, you don't have enough money to pay any more? Fine! Take a pass for this month. But next month when your bill comes (and every following month until it is paid off), pay at least what you paid this month. At the very minimum, lock your current minimum payment in as your budgeted monthly payment. Each month your credit card provider will reduce the minimum payment to 2% of the outstanding balance, but if you personally pledge to lock in a larger amount than that you will end up paying your card off much faster than you would if you just followed the bank's minimum-payment instructions.

Here is why. You've already seen that if you pay the aforementioned $5,000 debt off using the minimum payments provided by your credit card company (which will get lower and lower with time) it will take you approximately 32 years and 10 months to pay off what you owe. You'll also give the banks a profit of $11,898 in interest. On the other hand, if you lock in the current minimum payment of $100 it will only take you 7 years and 7 months to pay it off. Your total interest paid will then be reduced to $4,019, saving you $7,879. That's huge! By using this simple strategy in just over 7 years you could eliminate that debt and save enough money to buy a good used car in cash.

That's pretty exciting, isn't it? Hopefully now you can see the value in staying debt free and the folly in using credit cards to live beyond your true financial status. Let's take this example one step further and look at the real wealth impact of taking on $5,000 in credit card debt. (Hint: it's actually far greater than what we just looked at.)

Few people that have $5,000 worth of credit card debt could show you the assets they purchased with that money two years down the road. Maybe they could point to a television, stereo, or photo album of a trip they took, but more likely than not the debt was accumulated buying a bunch of little worthless things. Sure, those

THE REALITIES OF WEALTH TODAY

things may have some sort of value to you, but when it comes down to wealth, we need to look at the *real* value.

This is especially important when you are evaluating whether or not to take on debt for a purchase. I would estimate that two years after someone makes $5,000 worth of credit card charges, their retained value is no more than $1,000. If anything that was purchased is still around, the total value you would likely receive by selling them off would be less than $1,000. So that $5,000 you still owe is now offset by only $1,000 in assets, leaving your net worth down by a loss of $4,000. Had you held off on buying whatever you had to have and just contributed that money to a growth equity fund that managed a 10% return (which is still very possible in this market) your picture would have looked a lot different. Just look at the following two examples:

Fixed Payment Credit Card Payoff

Credit Card Expenditures: **$5,000**
Fixed Monthly Payment: **$100**
Total of Payments (Principal and Interest): **$9,019**
Indebted Period: **7 years and 7 months**
End Value of Items Purchased (if anything): **Less Than $1,000**

That's right, the total residual value of your $9,019 investment likely turns out to be less than $1,000.

Investing Debt Payment Equivalent
(investment at a 10% return)

Fixed Monthly Contribution: **$100**
Total of Investment: **$9,019**
Payment Period: **7 years and 7 months**
End Value of Investment: **$13,649**

The amount of free money earned just for making good decisions? A whopping $4,630. Now, here's the amazing part: the net wealth difference between the first example (the average American) and the second one (a wealth builder) is $12,649 in the wealth builder's favor. The sad part is that the average person will not likely pay off their debt in the 7 years and 7 months but rather ride repayment out for far longer (or in the worst case until they file bankruptcy).

Educate Kids Early About Money

If you have children (or are planning on having children), you have a moral obligation to pass on good wealth building habits to the next generation. The poorer your habits are the more important it is for you to break the cycle. In the past you may have had an excuse like, "I didn't know, so it's not my fault," but that got tossed out the window when you put your hands on The Wealth Builder Lifestyle.

Towards the end of this book is a section dedicated specifically to passing on the habits of a Wealth Builder Lifestyle to your children. Once you begin sharing this information with them, you will be amazed at how quickly they pick it up and the depths at which they understand it. Make it a point to share all the details about what we cover in this book. It can open up some great conversations and give them a head start on learning what they need to know about money to become successful.

Teach basic investing *now.* When the balance in a savings account reaches $1,000, show them how to open a custodial investment account. A good initial investment is a growth and income mutual fund. Teens can go online and research the performance and ratings to help choose their own investments.

Teach them early on about building their retirement. Waiting until that first full-time job to learn about investments and 401(k) plans is a mistake. The sooner they start saving for retirement, the more likely they will pick up good financial habits and reap the benefits of compound interest.

I'll go into greater detail later about the simple method I used to give my kids a head start on understanding money and wealth. It's simple, and yet very effective.

PART ONE:
CURRENT WEALTH STATUS

FINANCIAL STATUS TEST

Take a few minutes to go through this Financial Status Test. It will help you quickly analyze your situation to get an idea of your current financial lifestyle. Are you currently living as a super-charged wealth builder, or as a master of wealth destruction?

Date: ____/____/_____

Next to each section mark down a rating from 1 to 10 where 10 equates to being perfect, 5 is satisfactory—not bad, but not great—and 1 equates to being in serious need of improvement.

1) **Financial Security** – How close are you to having at least three months of expenses available in cash or liquid assets?	2) **Disability and Life Insurance** – Are you financially ready in the event of a surprise (such as a disability or death)?
3) **Assets** – Do you currently have an asset growth plan in place? Are you consistently increasing your assets?	4) **Spending** – Is your current spending lifestyle in balance? Are you currently living within your means?
5) **Budget** – Do you currently have (and follow) a budget? Does your lifestyle reflect financial discipline and a long-term plan?	6) **Short-Term Debt** – Is your credit card, auto, and other short-term debt minimal? Limiting your credit card use?
7) **Debt Elimination** – Are you currently debt free or working on a debt reduction plan?	8) **Career (Excluding Pay)** – Rate the fulfillment and enjoyment you get from your career and work environment.
9) **Income** – Is your income ideal? Put the number that represents the financial success of where you currently feel you are.	10) **Security Investments** – Are you currently saving an adequate percentage of your income in cash or secure investments?
11) **Growth Investments** – Do you have a strategy in place to consistently grow a portfolio of growth investments?	12) **Business Investments** – Do you have a high-growth investment strategy that will get you where you want to go?
13) **Net Worth** – Do you frequently track your net worth (what you own minus what you owe)? (10 - monthly, 1 - never)	14) **Environment** – Does your environment offer the career and lifestyle opportunities necessary to reach your
15) **Associations** – Are you surrounded with friends and colleagues that are supportive lifestyle role models?	16) **Knowledge** – Do you actively continue to grow your knowledge in your career, financial skills, and other aspects of life?
17) **Esteem** – Are you proud of your current career and financial status? Do you feel you are doing the best you can?	18) **Contribution** – Do you show gratitude for your successes by contributing back to others and society?
19) **Dream Lifestyle** – Are you currently financially capable of living your dream lifestyle while still building wealth?	20) **Fulfillment** – Is everything in your life adding up? Do you feel you are getting what you want out of life?

Scoring the Test

1. Add up all the individual scores you entered and write down your grand total.

2. Divide your grand total by two and then enter that number below as your score.

Grand Total _____   **Your Score**_____%

Change Your Status

So, how did you score? Maybe you are less than thrilled, and that's ok. It actually makes sense when you think about it. You internally knew you could be doing better—that's the whole reason why you picked up this program. The great news is that you've already made it this far, which says you are someone who will actually take the new actions necessary to improve your life. And you and I both know that change requires different actions. Look at anyone that is stuck and you will see that they continue to do the same things over and over (thus getting the same results). Even a small action that creates a little change has the potential to cause a ripple effect that can eventually lead to a major difference in outcome.

This is known as the "butterfly effect," which is really an amazing theory. If you have never heard of it or don't fully understand how it works, do a little research on the topic. Heck, there's even a movie called the *Butterfly Effect* with Ashton Kutcher in it that actually provides a great illustration of how even a minor change can affect the trajectory of your life in major ways you never thought possible.

On the following page take your three lowest scores and write the aspects to improve. These are the areas that you have the most room to improve in. Bringing these up just a few points will significantly improve your life. Write down some actions you can immediately take that will create significant changes in the areas you need to improve the most.

Three Major Target Areas to Improve:

1. Opportunity for Improvement: _____
    I will immediately take the following actions to improve this aspect
    of my life:

    _____

    _____

    _____

2. Opportunity for Improvement: _____
    I will immediately take the following actions to improve this aspect
    of my life:

    _____

    _____

    _____

3. Opportunity for Improvement: _____
    I will immediately take the following actions to improve this aspect
    of my life:

    _____

    _____

    _____

    Let's face it: money is a manmade essential need for modern life. In our contemporary world, not much happens without some kind of financial persuasion behind it. Managing money can be relatively easy, but there are still many forces working nonstop to reduce its value (and many more trying to find a way to get those dollars from you).

    We are going to begin by creating a snapshot of your current financial picture. Just follow the steps on the next page and fill in the worksheets to see exactly where you are. Most people are absolutely amazed when they get a clear picture of their current financial situation. For some, it's a good surprise and for others, it's a serious wake up call.

SPENDING

Although you can't just save your way to prosperity, being aware of your spending habits and refocusing some of your discretionary spending can greatly accelerate your wealth creation. Investing the value of just one $3 cup of coffee a day at a 10% return for the next 30 years would turn into $187,188. That means your total investment of $32,400, will have generated $154,788 in free wealth.

For the next 24 hours, challenge yourself to write down all of your discretionary expenses. Seriously! Don't just think about it. Carry a notepad in your pocket to note the item and cost of each of your purchases. At the end of the 24 hours, add up the total. Did it turn out to be more or less than you would have guessed?

You may not currently have all the information to fill out every category in this next form, but that's ok. Things like health, disability, and life insurance will be discussed in further detail on the following pages. If you don't currently have expenses that go into one of the categories, just leave it blank for now. You can always adjust it later if necessary. Any items not captured in one of the specific lines should be entered into the "Other" row of the corresponding category.

"You can't save your way to prosperity, but you can spend your way to poverty!"

- Daniel Hartjoy

PART ONE: CURRENT WEALTH STATUS

Work through the following calculations to establish your monthly minimum expenses.

Current Spending Expenses			
Housing Expenses		**Personal Expenses**	
Rent or mortgage	$ _____	Clothes	$ _____
Real Property Taxes	$ _____	Education	$ _____
Home/Renters Insurance	$ _____	Other Personal	$ _____
Maintenance and Repairs	$ _____	**Total Personal Expenses**	**$** _____
Other Housing	$ _____	**Fun Money Expenses**	
Total Housing	**$** _____	Entertainment	$ _____
Necessity Expenses		Travel and Gifts	$ _____
Utilities (All combined)	$ _____	Other Fun Stuff	$ _____
Health Insurance	$ _____	**Total Fun Money**	**$** _____
Disability Insurance	$ _____	**Short-Term Debt Expenses**	
Term Life Insurance	$ _____	Short-Term Debt	$ _____
Phones, Cable, Internet	$ _____	**Total Short-Term Debt**	**$** _____
Groceries and Household	$ _____		
Auto (all related expenses)	$ _____		
Laundry	$ _____	**Total Monthly Spending**	**$** _____
Other Necessity	$ _____		
Total Necessity	**$** _____		

Did you find any surprises in your spending habits? Sometimes just grouping and listing the items out can shed some light on potential areas of overspending. Often times we discover "sleeper" categories, or rather categories that we didn't realize we spend so much in. Sometimes just the discovery of these areas can get us motivated enough to make changes that can free up some money to apply towards a better use.

INCOME

Enter your monthly income information in the following form. If you only have the annual number, just divide it by twelve and input that amount. Our primary goal is to determine your net monthly income, so if you don't have your gross income numbers don't worry about it. Having them available can, however, be enlightening.

One of the not-so-secret secrets of the rich are tax shelters. These are used to reduce the amount of taxes that are paid on your gross income. This can in turn increase your net income or take-home pay without increasing your gross income. Essentially, this gives you a higher income without you having to actually earn more.

Current Monthly Income		
Income Source	Gross Income (before taxes)	Net Income (after taxes)
Wages and Tips	$	$
Long-Term Investments	$	$
High-Growth Investments	$	$
Business Investments	$	$
Property Investments	$	$
Refunds/Re-imbursements	$	$
Other Income	$	$
Total Income (all sources)	$	$

One sad fact of the financially undereducated is that they think raising taxes on the rich will somehow benefit them. The financially wise use tax shelters and loopholes to avoid paying these higher taxes, and any taxes they do have to pay will ultimately be passed on to employees through lower pay, reduced benefits, or (in the worst case) staff reductions. It's not an evil conspiracy, there's just no other way to pay for it. This is why the lowest-income earners always suffer from higher taxes. Either directly or indirectly, **the poorest people have always carried the tax burden,** regardless of which nation they call home. The solution is not more taxes, it's learning how to build wealth.

If you follow the Wealth Builder Lifestyle, you will be using some of these tax shelters to give you the same advantages. Higher taxes do not lead to increased wealth for the average person. Just look at the past. We consistently raise taxes and yet the rich and poor gap grows while poverty increases. It's a deception that simply doesn't work!

NOTES :

_____

_____

_____

_____

_____

_____

_____

_____

_____

_____

_____

_____

DEBT

As I demonstrated earlier, short-term debt is the archenemy of wealth building. This easy-to-obtain debt is like a virus and hard for many to shake. In most cases, short-term debt eats away at wealth faster than most wealth building techniques can create it, especially when compared dollar-for-dollar.

One of the best ways to jumpstart your wealth building plan is by paying off high-interest, short-term debt. Think about this: to break even with the financial losses created by $5,000 worth of credit card debt at an APR of 20%, you would need to have over $10,000 invested and earning a 10% annual return. The investment amount has to be so high because not only does it have to cover the amount lost to credit card debt interest, but also the income taxes (the ones I just spoke about) on your investment.

Use the next form to start forming a short-term debt-payoff plan. Start by entering your creditors, loan balances, and interest rates right off your last statements. Then comes the tricky part. Use a calculator to complete the following two formulas and fill in the last two columns.

Short-Term Debts

Monthly Interest – (Loan Balance × Interest Rate ÷ 12 = Monthly Interest)

Example loan: $3,500 × 0.16 = $560 ÷ 12 = $46.67 (0.16 equals 16 percent)

Monthly Principal – (Minimum Payment – Monthly Interest = Monthly Principal)

Example loan: $60.00 - $46.67 = $13.33

Current Short-Term Debts					
Creditor	Loan Balance	Interest Rate	Minimum Payment	Monthly Interest	Monthly Principal
Example Loan	*$3,500*	*16%*	*$60*	*$46.67*	*$13.33*
_____	$_____	____%	$_____	$_____	$_____
_____	$_____	____%	$_____	$_____	$_____
_____	$_____	____%	$_____	$_____	$_____
_____	$_____	____%	$_____	$_____	$_____
_____	$_____	____%	$_____	$_____	$_____
_____	$_____	____%	$_____	$_____	$_____
_____	$_____	____%	$_____	$_____	$_____
_____	$_____	____%	$_____	$_____	$_____
Combined Totals	$_____		$_____	$_____	$_____

If you need more space, make copies of this page as needed. Enter the combined total of all the columns (excluding the interest rate one). You'll be using this information later when creating your unique Twelve-Month Rebalance Blueprint.

Don't get discouraged. If you have made it this far you have taken more action than most, and like the saying goes, the first step is always the hardest. Congratulations, you've already taken it!

This program is like making some sweet apple pie. You have to put in time and effort, all the while making a mess that you'll have to clean up. But as you move along and the oven starts to billow out that amazing aroma, you know your efforts will soon pay off. When your fork finally breaks into that flakey crust, there will be no more doubt—it was all well worth it.

You're putting effort into your life that most people don't, and you will be rewarded.

SAVINGS AND INVESTMENTS

It's no wonder so many people in the United States are struggling financially. Without a good saving and investing plan, we dramatically limit our wealth-creation potential. Most people don't have the income and discipline necessary to save adequately for the future. A good saving and investment plan can help make up for any shortcomings in earning potential.

It's a sad reality, but many will eventually have to sell off everything they have worked their entire lives to build just to get by. Others will be in a position of giving up their independence, sacrificing their dignity, and having to ask for help from others to make up for their lack of a solid retirement strategy. You don't want or need to be either one of those statistics. Create and follow a Wealth Builder Lifestyle plan that will help ensure you can maintain your standard of living long after you lose your ability to work.

What are your current investing habits? This section is about your current investment lifestyle. The reason we call this your investment *lifestyle* is because your life is made up of habits. These habits determine your results, so we want to make sure your financial lifestyle is filled with good routines that will lead to a lifetime of wealth creation.

Let's take a look at your current investing habits. For some there may be nothing to fill in on this form. If that includes you, so be it. The past is the past, and you have the opportunity right now to create a better future. The point of investing is not about creating a better financial situation today. (That being said, every time you invest yours will be improving). It's really about planting the seeds that will eventually generate the wealth you will need down the road.

Unless you have a really high income, you likely do not have the ability to save enough money in your working lifetime to properly prepare for retirement. If by chance you do, you will likely suffer from a life of unnecessary sacrifice instead of one filled with abundance and prosperity. And who wants that?

In the following form, enter the amount you currently contribute to savings and investments. The following category descriptions will help you determine what type of investments you are presently making based on the Wealth Builder Lifestyle philosophy.

Security Investments

These are cash, precious metals, or other reasonably safe investments like your home, safer growth mutual funds, Certificates of Deposit, and other low-risk investments. These should be very safe with an annual return goal of approximately 7%.

Growth Investments

These are higher-return investments that are used to accelerate your wealth building which may be less liquid and have higher potential risk. They may include things like growth and income (as well as international) mutual funds (which can be reasonably safe investments that have potential for returns of 10% or higher).

Business Investments

These funds are used for your own personal business, investments directly into other companies, or things like more aggressive mutual funds. These will likely be higher-risk and have potential annual returns in excess of 15%.

NOTES:

_____

_____

_____

SAVINGS AND INVESTMENTS

Work through the following saving and investing habits form.

Current Savings and Investments			
Category	Combined Net Monthly Income	Average Monthly Contribution	Monthly Percentage Invested (contribution ÷ income)
Example Category	*$2,540*	*$150*	*6%*
Security Investments		$ _____	_____ %
Growth Investments	$ _____	$ _____	_____ %
Business Investments		$ _____	_____ %
Combined Savings and Investments		$ _____	_____ %

Do you currently feel you have an adequate investment strategy to prepare you for retirement and to cover you in the event of any unplanned setback? Yes ___ No ___

If not, what areas do you feel could use some improvement?

_____

_____

_____

How would you feel if (by taking the actions in this program) you were able to eliminate all of those areas of concern?

_____

_____

_____

How would your life be different, and what would it look like?

_____

_____

_____

PART ONE: CURRENT WEALTH STATUS

Saving and investing is not easy for most. I personally took a long time to come around, instead relying on growing my income to build wealth. That was foolish! As demonstrated earlier, there are lifecycles in wealth building and my choice in the long run will cost me substantial amounts of wealth. Instead of using my income as a strength and leveraging the investment lifecycle, I handicapped my overall wealth building power. As our financial education grows, so can our wealth. Learn from my mistakes—if you don't already invest, start now, not some day when you get around to it! Life moves too fast to take a chance on waiting.

FINANCIAL SECURITY CUSHION

Someday, it's going to rain. Don't get caught off guard. What I mean is, rarely do people have enough liquid wealth set aside to cover an unanticipated loss of income or other financial setback. This often leads to a rapid and excessive loss of wealth, damaged credit, or even bankruptcy. Everyone should have a plan to deal with an income interruption (preferably adequate enough to cover at least six months) using only cash and liquid assets.

A liquid asset is an asset that can be immediately converted into cash without substantial penalties. A non-liquid (or fixed) asset would be something like real estate, a car, a boat, or any other item that would take some time to convert to cash. Things like an IRA or 401K are not necessarily good liquid assets. Although you may be able to convert them into cash quickly, the taxes and penalties will only add to your financial setback.

NOTES :

_____

_____

_____

_____

_____

_____

_____

_____

PART ONE: CURRENT WEALTH STATUS

Before we move away from your current financial picture, perform the following calculations to determine how many months you could last without part or all of your current income. If you are in a dual-income household, evaluate the possible loss of one or both incomes.

Current Financial Security Cushion		
Option	Amount	Calculation
Example	*$2,500.00* -	← New Income
Cash & Liquid Assets	*$5,000.00* =	← Minimum Monthly Expenses
$7,500.00 ÷	-*$2,500.00* =	__3__ Months Without Income
Variation One	$_____ -	← New Income
Cash and Liquid Assets	$_____ =	← Minimum Monthly Expenses
$_____ ÷	$_____ =	_____ Months Without Income
Variation Two	$_____ -	← New Income
Cash and Liquid Assets	$_____ =	← Minimum Monthly Expenses
$_____ ÷	$_____ =	_____ Months Without Income

Regardless of your current situation, as you work through your custom plan we will make sure that you are building up an adequate security cushion. These things will not happen overnight, which is why I say that building wealth is a lifestyle and not just an event.

NOTES :

_____

_____

CURRENT NET WORTH

If you truly want to achieve a goal, you need to have a way to monitor and measure your progress. Everyone should know and continually monitor their net worth. Some financial gurus will advise you to primarily focus on your income and cash flow. I'm very fond of an approach that includes those aspects, but not in lieu of building your net worth and a diversified asset base.

If you're new to tracking your wealth (or are starting with little to no wealth/net worth), I would advise you to track your net worth monthly or quarterly at the very minimum. This may sound excessive, but being in tune and seeing even small movements in the right direction can help reaffirm your commitment and keep you focused.

The following page contains a form that will help you calculate your current net worth. You can make copies of this form or download a free copy by going to www.WealthBuilderLifestyle.com/tools.

The provided form is just one simple tool that can be a great gauge for accurately measuring your wealth. Think about this. Your car has numerous gauges just to tell you how it's doing, right? So doesn't it make sense that you would have a way to gauge and monitor one of the most important aspects of your life? Once you get in tune with your money, you will be amazed at how easy it is to hold on to and grow it.

Net Worth

Use the upcoming balance sheet to determine your net worth. Don't stress if you can't come up with a totally accurate amount for each category, just do the best you can. That being said, don't skip this task!

PART ONE: CURRENT WEALTH STATUS

Current Net Worth			
Assets (what you own)		**Liabilities** (what you owe)	
Property		**Property**	
Primary Residence	$_____	Primary Residence	$_____
Other Real Estate	$_____	Rental/Other	$_____
Planes, Boats, RVs	$_____	Planes, Boats, RVs	$_____
Vehicles	$_____	Other Real Property	$_____
Misc. Personal Property	$_____	Other	$_____
Furnishings	$_____	Other	$_____
Other	$_____	Other	$_____
Total Property	**$_____**	**Total Property**	**$_____**
Investments (security)		**Short-Term**	
IRA	$_____	Credit Cards	$_____
Bonds	$_____	Other	$_____
401K	$_____	**Total Short-Term**	**$_____**
Mutual Funds	$_____	**Total All Liabilities**	**$_____**
Stocks	$_____		
Other	$_____		
Total Security	**$_____**		
Investments (growth)			
401K	$_____		
Mutual Funds	$_____		
Stocks	$_____		
Other	$_____		
Total Growth	**$_____**		
Investments (business)			
Investment Property	$_____		
Other	$_____		
Other	$_____		
Total Business	**$_____**		
Savings (liquid assets)		**Total Net Worth**	
Savings Accounts (cash)	$_____	**Total Assets**	$_____
Metals	$_____	**Total Liabilities**	$_____
Other	$_____		
Total Savings	**$_____**	**TOTAL NET WORTH**	**$_____**
Total All Assets	**$_____**	(assets – liabilities = net worth)	

RETIREMENT PROGRESS CHART

Once you have established an accurate net worth, compare your net worth to the ideal wealth progress amount for your age group below. These numbers are here just to give you an idea of minimums you really want to be at in order to stay on track and reach the million dollar milestone.

Ideal Retirement Minimums					
Year	Balance	Year	Balance	Year	Balance
21	$3,815	36	$128,349	51	$542,802
22	$7,771	37	$143,977	52	$568,318
23	$12,152	38	$160,966	53	$595,121
24	$16,993	39	$179,420	54	$623,281
25	$22,333	40	$199,453	55	$652,872
26	$28,212	41	$221,187	56	$683,973
27	$34,676	42	$244,754	57	$716,666
28	$41,771	43	$270,294	58	$751,041
29	$49,550	44	$297,958	59	$787,191
30	$58,067	45	$327,908	60	$825,214
31	$67,383	46	$360,318	61	$865,216
32	$77,561	47	$395,375	62	$907,307
33	$88,670	48	$433,280	63	$951,606
34	$100,784	49	$474,247	64	$998,237
35	$113,981	50	$518,507	**65**	**$1,047,333**

Financial Stability

So, how did things look? Was your net worth as much as you thought it would be? Does your income adequately support your financial lifestyle?

MEETING NEEDS

Some of the "Needs" categories might not initially appear wealth-related, so here are a few examples that may help trigger the connection for you.

Sustenance

If your career or income is in doubt, you may be concerned you won't even be able to get by.

Connection

If you don't have a high enough income, you may not be able to afford the expenses related to spending time connecting with family and friends. Or worse yet, you may be putting these costs on credit cards.

Security

If you have very little saved and invested, you may feel on the edge and stressed out. You might even be worried that at any minute you could start falling behind and losing the wealth you've already created.

Growth

If you are not contributing to a savings and investment plan, you may feel like your financial status is stalled and not getting any better. This can lead to feelings of hopelessness.

Significance

If you have not built an acceptable amount of wealth for someone your age, you may feel like you are failing and or even insignificant.

Esteem

If your income has remained low and you have not, or are not, currently building wealth, you may feel inferior and like the world is looking down on you.

Inner Peace

If you don't have decent income, a good security cushion, growing investments, and a reasonable accumulation of assets for your age, you probably feel uncomfortable and rarely relax with peace of mind. In the applicable areas below, enter ratings of 1 to 10 with 10 indicating you are fully meeting your needs in that category at present.

How well are you meeting your Seven Human Needs in each area?						
Sustenance	Connection	Security	Growth	Significance	Esteem	Inner Peace
_____	_____	_____	_____	_____	_____	_____

Considering the current fulfillment of your human needs is one of the best ways to evaluate how you are doing financially. Not everyone needs the same amount of wealth or wealth building conditions to adequately meet their needs. Some people are content driving an old car and living in a humble home, while others would feel like they are total financial failures in that same situation. Those two people are going to have greatly different criteria for meeting their needs, and neither one is right or wrong. Everyone is wired differently, so we must all create a life that meets our own personal needs.

NOTES :

_____

_____

_____

_____

PART TWO:
TWELVE MONTH REBALANCE

,

RISK CONSIDERATIONS

Now that you have captured all of your current data, we need to setup some initial rules. Things like your age, whether you currently own or rent, how many kids you have, your marital status, and current income all greatly affect your strategy. These factors will influence your best plan of action for moving forward. Here are a couple example situations that we can compare for a closer look:

Single, 25, no kids

If you are 25, single, and have no kids, you have few limitations and the consequences of your actions are pretty low risk. If you lose your job (or everything you own, for that matter), you can probably sleep on a friend's couch and have plenty of time to recover. Alternatively, if you make some high-risk, high-reward moves, you may launch yourself into wealth at an early age.

Married, 40, with kids

If you are 40, rent your home, live in a single income household, have two teenage kids, and have limited savings, you are what I call high risk. If you lose your job, your family could end up homeless. Few people could easily take you in. You may need to move, change your kid's school, or worse just to recover. It would be a bad situation to say the least. In this type of situation, one wrong step could cause a lot of pain, so we need to be sure to do as much as we can to ensure that doesn't happen. Taking a high-risk, high-reward gamble at this point could be financially and mentally devastating, and the financial loss would likely be far easier for you to get over than the emotional trauma.

Calculated Risk

The following tools are going to give you recommendations based on the Wealth Builder Lifestyle method. These are only recommendations, and you need to make sure that they make sense for you. I'm an advocate of people being taught to think, not just *what* to think. These are conclusions based on what I think, so keep in mind that any decision you make has the potential for risk and reward. I personally like low-risk, high-reward situations, but then again there are no guarantees in life. If you work to protect yourself from every risk you may never be able to afford any opportunities to build wealth. You must find your own successful balance.

I believe you need to take calculated risks if you want to be rewarded. I also believe in hoping for the best but planning for the worst. I won't take on any potential upside if I'm not prepared and willing to suffer the downside.

There is a reason people in business have great opportunities and often reap great rewards. Contrary to popular belief, it's not because they steal or cheat people for money... They are just getting rewarded based on the risk they took and the value they created.

Those opportunities are available to anyone, but most just choose to take what is perceived as the low-risk method of working for someone else. Lower risk, perceived or real, typically equals lower pay, which reflects the amount of risk taken. If things go bad for an employee, they may lose their job and undergo financial hardship while they are finding a new one. If things go bad for a business owner, however, they may lose everything—business, home, credit, self-worth, the whole shebang. And after all that they could still end up being hundreds of thousands of dollars in debt. It's a risk/reward game: you decide how you want to play it.

Just keep in mind that if you are not building wealth, you are choosing a life of voluntary enslavement. You will always be owned by the people you have to pay to exist. The only way to truly be free is by obtaining a level of wealth that allows you to afford your own freedom.

RISK CONSIDERATIONS

Very few of even the elite, high-income earners can afford to buy their freedom with their career income. For everyone else, it will take time and a good plan to build the necessary level of wealth to ever be free. If you put off building wealth for absolute security today, you will run out of time and be at the mercy of your owners in the long run.

I know slavery is a strong word, and some may take offense, but I used it to get your attention. We are being lulled in to surrendering our freedom. As the cost of everything goes up (food, taxes, parking, rent, insurance), we have nothing left to dedicate to building wealth. This leaves us just working to exist without any luxuries or real freedom. This loss of freedom and opportunity has not come at the point of a gun, but unfortunately out of our own doing. Only we have the power to stop it.

NOTES :

_____

_____

_____

_____

_____

_____

_____

_____

_____

_____

_____

THE BOMB - INCOME ALLOCATIONS

You may not initially be able to meet all the program guidelines for your income allocations. That's not only okay, it's to be expected. These are your first set of goals, and this program is designed to help you work towards and then *eventually* meet them. The Wealth Builder Lifestyle front-loads your wealth building strategy in order to maximize your long-term results.

These numbers may appear aggressive or even impossible, but similar strategies that are even more aggressive have been used by many to successfully acquire millionaire and even billionaire status. A common trait that runs in many of the most successful in life is a habit of setting goals. I will help you define your focus and create a plan to successfully achieve all your financial goals.

Regardless of your income, these program principle goals will put you in a wealth building scenario. Each step you take from where you are towards being in line with these principles will make you a stronger wealth builder. It doesn't matter if you are currently going backwards, spending more than you are earning, or how much (if anything) you are saving and investing. Each step you take from here is a wealth builder step.

One thing is for sure: you're going to find out where you stand, which way you're currently moving, and how fast. After that's established we will work to shift you into a more powerful wealth building position. Small actions lead to big results, so don't get discouraged if your plan looks like a huge, insurmountable set of tasks. It may seem impossible for you to transition to a Wealth Builder Lifestyle, but have faith. You can absolutely do it.

PART TWO: TWELVE MONTH REBALANCE

Enter your total annual income (multiply monthly income from page 57 times twelve) in the form below to determine your income distributions.

Program Income Distribution Guidelines			
Select distribution percentages based on your income level.			
Annual Income	**Level 1**	**Level 2**	**Level 3**
$_____ Category	Up to $50,000	$50,000 to $150,000	$150,000 and above
Security Cushion Goal (percentage of income)	70%	60%	45%
Housing Expenses	45%	35%	25%
Necessity Expenses	15%	12.5%	10%
Personal Expenses	10%	10%	10%
Security Investments	10%	10%	15%
Growth Investments	10%	15%	15%
Business Investments	5%	10%	15%
Fun Money	5%	7.5%	10%
Short-Term Debt Payoff	(Varies)		
Reduce personal expenses and then investments to cover short-term debt payoff.			

As your income grows, so will the amount of each allocation. Over time it will become increasingly easier to meet these goals. Once you start investing, your investments will begin to create additional income which will contribute to your overall income.

Between 2007 and 2009, the average net worth of US households dropped by 23%. That's no insignificant amount! The global economy is in shambles and not surprisingly there is the potential for further decline. Some people will get financially hurt and some will never fully recover, but at the same time, others who seek out the unique opportunities created in this turmoil will accelerate their wealth creation faster than ever.

The government, investors, and businesses all need to keep money moving in order to make more of it. The economic crisis around the globe has put a lot of money on the move: some due to individuals searching for safe havens, some due to asset foreclosures, and more still thanks to business and personal bankruptcies. This "reshuffling of the deck" so to speak will create some great opportunities to purchase real estate and other assets at extremely low prices. Closing businesses will open up new doors for startups and market volatility will create opportunities for those that understand how to play it. Buckle down, be wise, and make sure this is a time of great prosperity for yourself and your family. There will be time to play when things stabilize later, but for now just get busy building wealth.

Your Income Allocation Totals

Take the percentages from the previous form that match your current income level and enter them in the following worksheet. Enter your net combined monthly income in the adjacent column and then multiply your monthly income by the percentage for each category.

You will need to start by determining the percentage required to pay the minimum payments on your current short-term debts. Then, reduce the Personal Expenses and long-term investment categories (followed by any others) as needed to balance all of the categories. For example, let's assume your net income is $2,000 and you have $150 in credit card debt you need to pay each month. Use this formula to determine the percentage of your income that needs to be dedicated to short-term debt. Divide the $150 by $2,000, then multiply that answer by 100 to determine the percentage: $150 ÷ $2,000 = 0.075. By multiplying that value (0.075) by 100, you can find the required percentage is 7.5%.

NOTES :

_____

_____

_____

Current Program Income Distribution Guidelines			
Distribution Category	Your Percentages	Net Monthly Income	Monthly Allowance (income × percentage)
Example Category	*20%* ×	*$2,000* =	*$400*
Housing Expenses	_____ % ×		$ _____
Necessity Expenses	_____ % ×		$ _____
Personal Expenses	_____ % ×		$ _____
Security Investments	_____ % ×	$ _____ =	$ _____
Growth Investments	_____ % ×		$ _____
Business Investments	_____ % ×		$ _____
Fun Money	_____ % ×		$ _____
Short-Term Debt Payoff	_____ % ×		$ _____
Grand Total (be sure not to exceed 100%)			$ _____

Have you caught your breath yet? You're probably wondering what you were thinking, wanting to retire a millionaire. Starting at ground zero, this can seem overwhelming (if not totally impossible). Depending on your initial financial situation, this may just take some getting used to or it might require substantial cuts and life changes. In the following pages we will work through a multi-faceted, twelve month transition plan that will get you from point A to point B.

Once you get some time under your belt implementing these strategies, you will start to see dramatic improvements in your financial situation. These initial improvements will show up and be the most apparent in your net worth. You will also begin to see impressive growth in your financial statements, especially if you are starting from zero and have never had any investment accounts before.

Saving and investing may seem out of your league if you are not somewhat financially savvy. But amazingly, in these financially complex times it has actually never been easier because there are currently so many different investment options and opportunities.

Once you have crossed the line and made your first few investments, you will feel much more confident and relaxed. This is something absolutely anyone can do!

If you are an experienced investor, this may include little more than tuning up your investment strategy, becoming a more aggressive investor, or just redistributing some investment assets into safer, more balanced allocations.

Where to Apply These Allocations

Meeting these goals will likely require some initial lifestyle adjustments. Just remember, we are talking about changing a life from one that spends the last 20 to 30 years struggling stressfully to one of financial security and comfort. Take a moment to visualize your retirement life down the road if you continue on your same course. The assurances provided by being financially sound should easily offset the initial discomfort. Here is the breakdown of what these allocations specifically cover.

Housing Expenses

This allowance will be used to cover your rent or home loan payments and other direct housing-related expenses like insurance, maintenance, and so on.

Necessity Expenses

All utility, phone, auto, grocery, child, health, disability, and insurance costs are included in this category.

Personal Expenses

These funds will be used for all your personal expenses such as haircuts, gym memberships, higher education, clothing, short-term loans, and any other personal items.

Security Investments

These investments should include low-risk assets like real estate, safer mutual funds, Certificates of Deposit, and possibly even a 50/50 allocation in cash and precious metals. Your goal is to try to get a safe 7% return. You should maintain enough of these in fairly liquid assets for use as your security cushion.

Growth Investments

This allocation will go towards higher return investments which may be less liquid and have higher potential risks. These will likely include growth, income, and international mutual funds as well as other investments that are not overly risky but have potential for returns in excess of 10%.

Business Investments

These funds may be used to invest directly in your own business or other companies. These will have higher anticipated returns in excess of 15% and (inherently) higher risk.

Fun Money

This is your reward. After all, all work and no play is no way to live. It's important that you actually spend this money to reward yourself or your family for following your plan. Don't try to be a superstar and invest or save this money. It may sound silly, but you have a far higher chance of failure if you don't focus this money on a fun reward because you could end up burning yourself out.

Short-Term Debt Payoff

Our goal is to get you to carry little to no short-term debt, especially in the early stages. Initially, you'll probably need to divert money from other areas in an amount that is adequate to meet your debt-reduction plan total. We will determine that exact amount later.

There may come a time when you need to violate the recommended percentages and reallocate some funds to balance your finances, and that's ok. But try to avoid it as much as possible. The problem created by repeatedly moving the boundaries is that they begin to lose their strength and you can actually start to develop new bad habits (and that works against our intention of creating positive Wealth Builder Lifestyle habits).

Shock Reduction

These days, a large percentage of our population is living closer and closer to the edge, if you find yourself a part of that statistic, don't be too hard on yourself. It should come as no surprise these days as we are bombarded with powerful, psychologically-driven advertisements and social pressure to appear wealthy (regardless of whether we actually are). This keeps us in debt and spending money rather than investing and doing the things that actually lead to being truly wealthy.

With so little emphasis placed on good financial education, most people are not prepared to fight off all the powerful forces pursuing their dollars. These efforts are in full force, coming from all angles—businesses, family, friends, and even the government. As your income and spending go up, the revenue the government earns through taxes automatically increases. Yet the government continues to raise tax rates to cover their poor financial habits. This continues to reduce the amount of money we have available to invest and spend, so we need to earn more and more just to stay in the same spot. If you're not actively growing your income and investments, you'll inevitably fall behind.

One of the great things about the Wealth Builder Lifestyle is that it not only focuses on solid spending and investment strategies but it also provides you with multiple strategies for career development and career income growth. By incorporating accelerated career income growth into your Wealth Builder Lifestyle you can put your overall wealth creation into hyper drive.

PART TWO: TWELVE MONTH REBALANCE

It's easy for people to fall into certain careers or feel like they have no other opportunities. This is where a mentor can help open your mind to new ideas. Taking action on a good career development plan can almost immediately lead to increased income, creating substantial increases within one to two years and having a tremendous effect on your lifetime earning potential.

I have personally used the same strategies I'm going to share with you to increase my own income multiple times by large percentages (and even doubled it a few times). I certainly can't guarantee these results for you, but I also never would have thought them possible for me—that is, until I met my unintentional mentor. Since I grew up poor, I was not naturally in an environment of wealth and thus had no idea how the real world of money worked. I got lucky and met a guy that had the skills necessary for life and career advancement who would eventually become a great friend and (ultimately) an unintentional, life-long mentor.

You see, I was raised up under the idea that you had to work hard for your money (and hard usually meant difficult physical labor). I still believe you have to work hard, but there is much more to it these days. Today, what is far more important is the market value that your energy produces. When you learn to create value, you give yourself leverage to move up. Then you need the confidence to emanate that value so you can sell it when it counts. This may come from getting something you don't already have (such as professional training) or it may come from just understanding the true value you already hold. We'll get into that more shortly.

NOTES :

_____

_____

_____

Twelve-Month Rebalance Plan

We have done some initial investigation into your current financial situation, so now let's break that information down and create a realistic plan that can transition you from where you are to within the Wealth Builder Lifestyle principles.

I'm not going to mislead you and say that this will be easy or even painless. The reality is more likely than not it will be a challenge, at least initially. The good part is that once you become balanced you will be living a life of prosperity instead of under a false illusion of wealth. The Wealth Builder Lifestyle is not like a crazy diet where you constantly live in an extreme state, it's simply a lifestyle of habitual wealth creation. Once you figure that out and find your balance, it will just be the way you live and perpetual wealth creation will be a default byproduct of your lifestyle.

You will be going against the popular trend of lifestyles filled with reckless spending and excessive debt, both personally and governmentally. What you will be doing will likely feel foreign to you and appear foreign to the majority of people around you. The other side of that coin is that the people that *do* understand your actions will be some of the wealthiest people in the world. It doesn't matter where you are starting from or how much wealth you currently have—that demographic does not exclude you. Your current situation just determines your starting point.

The point of a twelve month rebalancing plan is to get the painful part of the system out of the way as soon as possible. If the sacrifices are ongoing, the chances of you sticking with it diminish drastically. That being said, taking an approach that is too discreet could potentially harm your chances by not stirring you up enough to keep you focused on the goal. The danger there is that it can allow you to slip back into old habits, leading to another failed attempt at lifestyle change. The more difficult the rebalancing period, the more necessary it was and the more you should be proud of the actions you are taking.

PART TWO: TWELVE MONTH REBALANCE

I wish I could say most people could just step in with no rebalancing and get on their way. Unfortunately, the statistics of our population prove contrary to this wish for the majority of people. As I sit here writing this, the need for people to take personal responsibility for their financial wellbeing is becoming more and more necessary. I have no expectations of our global economy returning to boom times anytime soon, and those that are waiting for good times to roll around before strengthening their own financial situations are going to get hurt the most.

Like I mentioned earlier, I am someone that advises people to hope for the best and plan for the worst. The principles of the Wealth Builder Lifestyle are designed with that in mind. If things go great, your wealth will just grow faster. If, on the other hand, things go poorly, you will be prepared as well as is reasonably possible. We all watched highly-respected "financial experts" advise people not to panic or take their money out of the stock market back in 2008 only to see the Dow Jones Industrial Average collapse from 13,000 to 6,600. The people that listened to that advice sustained huge losses and many I know have, unfortunately, never fully recovered.

I don't say this to discourage you by any means. Rather, my goal is just the opposite. I want you to be motivated to get informed, get a plan, and protect yourself financially as soon as possible. I don't want you to be a victim of the so-called experts' advice. Most people knew in their gut that something was wrong but relied on others to make their financial decisions. Those people didn't understand money enough to avoid the losses. Let's learn from the situation and not make that mistake again. You don't have to know everything about money to be a wealth builder, but you do need to have a strategic plan based on sound principles.

We will now work to establish your rebalancing plan, this will create a foundation and starting point for you to start building wealth from.

THE BOMB - INCOME ALLOCATIONS

Enter the Total Income (all sources) you determined on page 57 in the boxes below.

Current Monthly Income		
Income	Gross Monthly Income (before taxes)	Net Monthly Income (after taxes)
Total Income (all sources)	$_____	$_____

NOTES :

_____

_____

_____

_____

_____

_____

_____

_____

_____

_____

_____

_____

_____

_____

_____

_____

_____

_____

BAD HABIT ASSESSMENT

When it comes to building wealth, two of the hardest habits to control are how much you spend and how much you invest. We indulge in spending for instant gratification and put off investing while we wait for some mysterious future date when the time will be right. Unfortunately, that date and time never seems to come in time (or even at all, for most).

Well, I've got the mysterious, fail-safe time you have been waiting for, and I'm going to finally reveal this once elusive secret: the time is **now!**

Complete the following two worksheets to determine how much of an adjustment you will need to make in each category. This will determine exactly what it will take to get from where you are currently to within the Wealth Builder Lifestyle guidelines. Most of this information you have already captured, so you can refer back to the corresponding pages listed below for your answers. As a note, we will initially use your Combined Minimum Payment Total for your short-term debt before determining how much money it makes sense to free up in order to accelerate paying these debts off.

Current Spending Expenses table -- Page 56.

Current Short-Term Debts table -- Page 60.

Current Savings and Investments table -- Page 63.

Current Program Income Distribution Guidelines table -- Page 82.

Spending Habits

In the following form, enter the actual amount you are currently paying and the principle guideline amount for each item in the corresponding columns and categories. To determine the net difference between what you pay towards each category and what the principle advises, use the following formula:

actual amount - guideline amount = net difference

Then add and subtract all the category totals to determine the cumulative net difference for all your spending categories.

Note: for your "Guideline" and "Net Difference" you do not need to break down each item individually. These spaces have been provided as an option, to help you better budget and focus in on individual areas that could be adjusted to help meet your overall guideline goals.

NOTES :

_____

_____

_____

_____

_____

_____

_____

_____

_____

_____

BAD HABIT ASSESSMENT

Spending Habits (Twelve-Month Rebalance)			
Housing Expenses	**Actual Amount**	**Guideline**	**Net Difference**
Example	*$75.00*	*$100.00*	*$-25.00*
Home (rent or mortgage)	$_____	$_____	$_____
Property Taxes (if separate)	$_____	$_____	$_____
Home/Renter's Insurance	$_____	$_____	$_____
Maintenance/Other	$_____	$_____	$_____
Total Housing Expenses	$_____	$_____	$_____
Necessity Expenses	**Actual Amount**	**Guideline**	**Net Difference**
Utilities (all combined)	$_____	$_____	$_____
Health Insurance	$_____	$_____	$_____
Disability Insurance	$_____	$_____	$_____
Term Life Insurance	$_____	$_____	$_____
Phone, Cable, Internet	$_____	$_____	$_____
Auto (all related expenses)	$_____	$_____	$_____
Groceries and Household	$_____	$_____	$_____
Child Care	$_____	$_____	$_____
Laundry, Other	$_____	$_____	$_____
Total Necessity Expenses	$_____	$_____	$_____
Personal Expenses	**Actual Amount**	**Guideline**	**Net Difference**
Clothes	$_____	$_____	$_____
Education	$_____	$_____	$_____
Other	$_____	$_____	$_____
Total Personal Expenses	$_____	$_____	$_____
Fun Money	**Actual Amount**	**Guideline**	**Net Difference**
Entertainment	$_____	$_____	$_____
Vacations, Travel, Gifts	$_____	$_____	$_____
Other	$_____	$_____	$_____
Total Fun Money	$_____	$_____	$_____
Net Surplus or Deficit	**Actual Amount**	**Guideline**	**Net Difference**
Grand Totals	$_____	$_____	$_____

INVESTING HABITS

Enter the actual amount you are currently investing and the principle guideline amount for each item in the corresponding column for each category. To determine the net difference between what you invest in each category and what the principles advise use the following formula:

actual amount - principle guideline amount = net difference

Investing Habits (Twelve-Month Rebalance)			
Investments	Actual Amount	Guideline	Net Difference
Example	*$75.00*	*$100.00*	*$-25.00*
Security Investments	$_____	$_____	$_____
Growth Investments	$_____	$_____	$_____
Business Investments	$_____	$_____	$_____
Total Investments	**$_____**	**$_____**	**$_____**
Short-Term Debt Payoff			
Short-Term Debt Payoff	$_____	$_____	$_____
Net Surplus or Deficit			
Total Investments and Debt Payoff	$_____	$_____	$_____

Complete the following recap using your category totals to create a simplified overview of your spending and investing habits. Then, add your spending totals to your investing totals to determine your combined net surplus or deficit. If your actual amount exceeds the principle guideline (which should equal your total income), then you are spending more than you are earning. Unless you have some great investments, you are likely eroding wealth monthly rather than increasing it.

PART TWO: TWELVE MONTH REBALANCE

Spending and Investment Totals (Twelve-Month Rebalance)			
Spending	Actual Amount	Guideline	Net Difference
Total Housing Expenses	$_____	$_____	$_____
Total Necessity Expenses	$_____	$_____	$_____
Total Personal Expenses	$_____	$_____	$_____
Total Fun Money Spending	$_____	$_____	$_____
Total Spending (all categories)	**$**_____	**$**_____	**$**_____
Savings and Investments			
Total Savings and Investments	$_____	$_____	$_____
Total Short-Term Debt Payoff	$_____	$_____	$_____
Total Investments (all categories)	**$**_____	**$**_____	**$**_____
Net Surplus or Deficit			
Grand Totals	**$**_____	**$**_____	**$**_____

You may feel like some of these exercises are redundant, but remember that we are trying to build familiarity with working with money and an acute awareness of your own personal financial situation. This will help you build a subconscious awareness of where you currently are and what you need to do to start living a successful lifestyle full of wealth building habits. Having this awareness and understanding greatly increases your chance for successfully creating lasting change.

Are you actually spending more each month than you make? Are you anywhere close to being in line with the principle guidelines for your income? If you are, congratulations! You are one of few, and the rest of this program should come easy for you. The beauty is that by this point you should be able to identify where you need to make the biggest changes in order to transition into a Wealth Building Lifestyle.

So far, we have really covered the basics via a general analysis of where you currently are compared to where you need to be to start habitually creating wealth. That is a great first step, but now we need to

INVESTING HABITS

start looking for the easiest areas to make the most significant changes to get you onto the fast track. During the initial rebalancing phase, we are going to work primarily with things that you currently have direct control over and can change immediately. We will use these initial changes to leverage larger overall changes that will get you in your best possible position for maximum lifetime wealth creation.

NOTES :

_____

_____

_____

_____

_____

_____

_____

_____

_____

_____

_____

_____

_____

_____

_____

FINANCIAL SECURITY INSURANCE

Use the following forms to calculate some risk variables based on the Wealth Builder Lifestyle. All the options we will be looking at have merit, but the question of whether or not you can afford to purchase them (and when each choice makes sense) is one you'll have to answer yourself.

Health Insurance

By the time you read this you may have already lost your freedom of choice. You may have no option other than to pay what you are told to for health insurance or shell out a fine.

The idea of health insurance is great—and in a perfect world we should all have it—but in reality if you are under 30 the likelihood of you having a medical need that makes it financially sensible goes way down (especially if you can't afford it while building wealth).

If you took the money that you would pay in premiums for insurance coverage from the age of 18 until 30 and invested it, you would have a sizable investment. Unlike the fear-building political speak, in the unlikely event that you did have a medical expense you would likely have enough money to cover your expenditures out of pocket and in cash.

NOTES :

_____

_____

_____

PART TWO: TWELVE MONTH REBALANCE

If you are like me, that may not really paint a clear picture. Personally, I need to see things clearly—which is why I created this program. In the following evaluation, the last amount (year 35) is based on just leaving the investment to grow after 12 years with no further contributions. The table below should help paint a more comprehendible picture and make it easier to understand the numbers behind health insurance. It gives a comparison of insurance premiums versus an equivalent investment at a 10% rate of return over time.

Health Insurance Versus Investment				
Premium Invested	$100	$150	$200	$250
Year 1	$1,264	$1,896	$2,528	$3,160
Year 2	$2,655	$3,982	$5,309	$6,636
Year 3	$4,184	$6,276	$8,368	$10,460
Year 4	$5,866	$8,800	$11,733	$14,666
Year 5	$7,717	$11,576	$15,434	$19,293
Year 6	$9,753	$14,629	$19,506	$24,382
Year 7	$11,992	$17,988	$23,985	$29,981
Year 8	$14,456	$21,683	$28,911	$36,139
Year 9	$17,165	$25,748	$34,330	$42,913
Year 10	$20,146	$30,219	$40,292	$50,364
Year 11	$23,424	$35,137	$46,849	$58,561
Year 12	$27,031	$40,546	$54,062	$67,577
Year 35	$242,044	$363,061	$484,088	$605,105
Buy Insurance	This one is easy to calculate. Your return will always be $0!			

While you age and become more likely to develop medical needs, your account is growing into a more sizable and capable fund. The odds say that you would end that time period with most (if not all) of your investment in tact, a great head start at building wealth. If you take the opposite approach and pay the premiums, at the end of 12 years you will have nothing. I'm not telling you which way to go, I just believe in people having good, unbiased information and then making their own decisions.

FINANCIAL SECURITY INSURANCE

After 30, the chance that you will have healthcare-related needs goes up, so whether you invest and pay out of pocket or buy insurance and they pay becomes less important. Either way, you will have a cost and these numbers may become a wash. Keep in mind, I promote running your life as a business, and an insurance company is a business. Your premiums are based on them calculating the risk and the likelihood that they will have to pay out. Then they charge you not only to cover the money they will pay out, but also for their advertising costs, administration expenditures, and so on.

In the end, no matter how you slice it we are paying all the costs. But if you get ahead of the curve early, your investment account could be larger than the insurance benefits would pay, regardless of the premium. If you do invest and get to that point, you are in a position to really ratchet up your investing and explode your wealth. Should you not have any major medical expenses until you are older, you will likely be sitting on a good fortune.

Think about it. We are always complaining about how much profit the insurance companies are making and how crappy their care is. It's no wonder! Our premiums are going into advertising, profits, overhead, lobbying, and all kinds of other costs that don't improve the care we actually receive.

Keep in mind, the numbers I used were also low premium numbers that you likely can only get while you are young and healthy. Health insurance premiums are skyrocketing and as you get older you could easily be paying $400 to $600 (to even $800 or more) a month. Investing those amounts would create rapid wealth creation.

Who Wants to Be a Millionaire?

If we look at just the $250 investment amount, over the 35 years at 10% your total nest egg would be a whopping $605,105. That's not fluff. Those are real, achievable numbers that any financial expert can verify for you. Keep in mind that I've only outlined twelve years of making contributions, accounting for just letting it sit and grow for the rest of the time. So by the time someone is 30, they could have this seed planted and be setup with a great start on a fully-funded retirement without any further contributions.

If you took that same $250 premium and paid it from age 20 until 65 (essentially what you will do when buying insurance, although your insurance rate will shoot way beyond that as you age) the total investment you would have at 65 would be $2,271,836. I know, I know, we need to figure some medical costs in there, but come on—I'm sure you can afford it.

At this point (unless something changes), it doesn't appear that you will have any other choice than to pay the insurance companies so they can build their wealth. A disgrace, really. Unless the same people who are taking away your choice and limiting your ability to build wealth for yourself are willing to guarantee you prosperity and financial security through the end of your life (which they can't), I think you deserve to have the right to choose.

There are reasons why the poor in this country are getting poorer and the rich are getting richer. Taking away peoples' rights to chose is a huge step towards ensuring more people join the ranks of the poverty stricken. I'm not trying to get political here, but this will have a huge impact on the average person's ability to build wealth and take care of themselves.

The following Health Insurance Evaluator will be very controversial because recommending someone at age 50 go without insurance won't sit well with some. I truly wouldn't want to see anyone at age 50 without health insurance, but I think that having less than $100,000 in net worth at that time is a far bigger risk to your wellbeing than not having health insurance.

Check your age, income, and net worth for a specialized recommendation. The calculations are based on an individual. If you are a couple, double all of the variables. If your recommendation is Ins./**Inv.**, refer to the "Retirement Progress Chart" on page 69. If you find that you have reached or exceeded the ideal retirement progress for your age, get insurance, if you are still below it you should consider investing.

Health Insurance Evaluator					
Income	Net Worth	Age 18 to 30	Age 30 to 40	Age 40 to 50	Age 50+
Less than $50,000	Less than $50,000	Invest	Invest	Invest	Invest
	Over $50,000	Insurance	Ins./Inv.	Ins./Inv.	Ins./Inv.
$50,000 to $150,000	Less than $50,000	Invest	Invest	Invest	Invest
	$50,000 to $150,000	Insurance	Ins./Inv.	Invest	Invest
	Over $150,000	Insurance	Insurance	Ins./Inv.	Ins./Inv.
Over $150,000	Less than $150,000	Insurance	Ins./Inv.	Invest	Invest
	Over $150,000	Insurance	Insurance	Ins./Inv.	Insurance

Kids should always be insured if possible. For low income families, there are usually government programs available at low or no cost. If you have children that are not currently insured, do some research and find out what the most affordable solution is for you. Regardless of whether you follow this guideline or not, enter your anticipated monthly premium below (if you plan to carry health insurance). You can get an estimated premium online if needed.

Monthly Health Premium	$ _____

Disability Insurance

In the event you are unable to work due to a sickness or injury, disability insurance can provide some assurance that you will be able to continue paying your bills while maintaining your lifestyle. The premiums for this type of insurance typically run between 1 to 3% of your annual income. There are two scenarios when this type of insurance has substantial value.

Limited Cash Reserves

If you are financially close to the edge (meaning you do not have enough money in your security cushion to cover all your expenses for at least six months), this type of insurance may be a great option for you. If nothing else, it may be a good temporary fallback plan until you can adequately fund your security cushion.

Sole Provider

If you are the sole provider for your family and you get injured, you could put your family's livelihood at risk and potentially cause stress and hardship that could've easily been avoided.

If you aren't prepared to cover your expenses in the event of an emergency, you may also be putting your assets at risk with the potential to lose more than just your income. Consider this. If you have a $200,000 home with a mortgage balance of $125,000, you have $75,000 in equity. Should you fall behind and miss a few months of payments, your bank has the legal right to foreclose on your property. This means you could not only lose your home but also that $75,000 in equity.

This same situation could also come into play on any other assets that you currently have loans on. If you are considering getting disability insurance, take some time to review all your current loans. Some credit cards and other loans may already include coverage for your payments in the event of a disability. **Note:** if this is an optional feature they're going to charge you for, it's usually less expensive to cover this risk with a separate umbrella disability insurance policy. Don't make the pricey mistake of insuring these risks with multiple layers of coverage.

The length of time you will receive coverage will depend on whether you get a short- or long-term policy. You'll want to make sure that your coverage will extend at least long enough to give you adequate time to sell or make other arrangements to protect your assets.

You can easily find places online that can give you a quote for this type of insurance. That being said, if you are seriously considering this insurance, I advise talking to someone in person before you purchase it. That way you can make sure you fully understand the coverage you will be receiving.

You will want to make sure you get at least enough coverage to pay your monthly minimum expenses. Then determine the duration of time you would like to be protected for.

If you will be obtaining disability insurance, enter your anticipated premium here:

Monthly Disability Premium	$ _____

Term Life Insurance

If you or your spouse are unfortunate enough to suffer a tragedy, term life insurance can be a huge relief. It's relatively inexpensive and can make a world of difference in a bad situation. Keep in mind that once a certain level of wealth is reached, term life insurance may not be as essential but might still make good financial sense.

If this type of coverage makes sense for you, use the following formula to determine your Wealth Builder Lifestyle guideline for term life insurance. The word "estate" in the following chart means that you have a reasonable amount of assets that need to be protected or paid off to keep your estate settlement safe and simple.

	Term Life Insurance Evaluator					
Description	**Single** no kids or estate	**Single** kids or estate	**Married** single income	**Married** dual income	**Enter** **Children**	**Total** **Coverage**
Income	N/A	$____	$____	$____	N/A	Combine all column totals to determine amount of coverage.
Quantity	1	N/A	N/A	N/A	____	
	×	×	×	×	×	
	$25,000	5	10	5	$100,000	
	=	=	=	=	=	
Category Total	$____	$____	$____	$____	$____	$____

The total you came up with working through this form is what I believe to be a safe amount of coverage. Single individuals with little to no assets really don't have a big need for coverage. The reason I still believe this is a good idea is due to the fact that it's very affordable. Plus, in the event of a death you would not be adding a financial burden onto others (who will already be enduring a terrible situation).

Some advise death benefits for single individuals more in the range of $10,000, but for the nominal premium increase I advise $25,000. This provides some additional cash to resolve any outstanding issues and can just help the situation go smoother in general.

Similarly, I advise a higher multiple of income for married couples with single incomes. The primary reason for this is because if one person is not working they are typically losing income-earning value by not increasing or maintaining their career skills. In the event of a death, they will not only be forced to pick up the financial responsibilities but will also have to do it with what could be a severe disadvantage. This is one reason (in cases of divorce) that the courts typically order support for the non-working spouse.

If you will be obtaining term life insurance, enter your anticipated premium here:

Monthly Term Life Premium	$ _____

Insurance Summary

Insurance can be great when you need it, but it's also a product. Companies tend to want to sell it to everyone, often regardless of whether it is in the purchaser's best interest or not. It is up to us as individuals to be informed consumers and make our own best decisions.

Based on the decisions you made on the last few pages, enter all your monthly premiums in the next form. Then combine your health, disability, and term life insurance premiums and enter the total.

Monthly Insurance Premiums	
Health Insurance	$ _____
Disability Insurance	$ _____
Term Life Insurance	$ _____
Total Monthly Premiums	**$ _____**

Security Cushion

As much as we may want to get aggressive paying off your debt and getting your money working for you, it would be foolish to do this with reckless abandon. I know many people that live right on the edge with no cushion for life's little surprises, and that's not a wise decision.

I'm not just talking about those with limited incomes. I'm also talking about very wealthy people. It's easy to look at wealthy people and say they have it made with nothing to worry about, but few consider the fact that they are often some of the most vulnerable to unexpected changes in their incomes or the economy. How could this be true? The only difference between wealthy and poor people without a good financial security plan is that the former have a bigger ship to crash. Things can unravel every bit as fast for them as those of average means, and often times even faster.

How long could you last if you had to come up with, say, an extra $30,000 a month? That's a bit of a crazy question, right? Well, many of the people that we see as rich have control of things like commercial properties which may have huge loans to pay on or businesses that they will have to cover any shortages for during a slowdown. If the economy slows down, they might lose a renter and the associated income. In a case like that, they may need to come up with that $30,000 shortage personally. That reduction could easily last twelve months in a row, turning into $360,000 over a year. That is a huge loss, even for someone with great wealth. That sort of downturn won't take long to destroy even a substantial amount of wealth.

What can compound this loss of wealth (regardless of how much you have) is the lack of an adequate financial security cushion. Should you stumble upon a hard time and not be able to pay that $30,000—or whatever your shortage is per month—you could quickly fall behind on loan payments such as your home, investment properties, cars, or other assets. This could lead to foreclosure or repossession, regardless of how much equity you have in these assets. That's how your perceived wealth can vanish in only a moment. Instead of just losing $360,000 in a year, you could lose a million or more. These figures are hypothetical, of course, but this scenario is not only real, it's frequently taking place throughout the good times and bad.

So, regardless of how much wealth you have, you need to have a plan in place to avoid being put into that type of situation. Keep in mind, when you are down and have something like this come up, people and banks will abandon you without a second thought. If you lose your income or have another financial hardship, your ability to borrow your way out of it will likely vanish as quickly as the problem arose.

Ultimately you will want to build a fully funded twelve month security cushion, but for now let's just make sure you have at least a bare minimum cushion in place. I strongly recommend you have and maintain at least one month of your minimum expenses in cash or other liquid assets that you do not touch. As you pay down your short-term debt, you should have more available credit to cover you in an emergency, so we will not look to build up the ultimate security cushion until your short-term debt is at least substantially eliminated.

Enter the amount of your minimum monthly expenses from page 96 in the box below:

One Month Security Cushion	$ _____

If you already have enough set aside to cover your one month security cushion, great! Leave that alone and don't touch it. If, on the other hand, you don't, we need to create a plan to build that cushion over the next twelve months while still freeing up money to accelerate your short-term debt payoff.

Use the following worksheet to determine the amount you need to set aside each month to build your security cushion. This should be done simultaneously with the scheduled debt reduction, not one now and then the other later. The reason for this is because we want forward progress and good habits to be built beginning right *now*. If you do one first and then the other afterward, by the time you finish number one you may have forgotten all about the other.

NOTES :

_____

_____

_____

_____

_____

_____

_____

_____

PART TWO: TWELVE MONTH REBALANCE

Follow the steps below to determine the monthly amount to set aside for your security cushion.

Security Cushion Calculator (Twelve-Month Rebalance)		
Enter Amounts	**Description**	**Monthly Security Cushion Contribution**
_$1,750.00_ - _$600.00_ =	← One Month Security Cushion ← Current Cash or Liquid Assets	_Example_
_$1,150.00_ ÷	12	= _$95.83_
$_____ - $_____ =	← One Month Security Cushion (from above) ← Current Cash or Liquid Assets	**Your Plan**
$_____ ÷	12	= $_____

During the Twelve-Month Rebalance phase of the program, you may need to sacrifice some of the program's guideline investment contributions. This is necessary to make sure that you substantially reduce or eliminate your short-term debt and build up your security cushion. We don't want to totally eliminate your investment contributions because we are trying to establish well-balanced Wealth Builder Lifestyle habits (so the sooner we make investments a habitual part of your lifestyle the better).

By repeatedly taking good financial actions, you'll be building habits that will allow you to create a lasting Wealth Builder Lifestyle. What takes conscious thought and sacrifice today will become your natural response in time, which will in turn keep your wealth growing by default.

SPENDING ALIGNMENT

The government says, "We can't cut spending to reduce our debt and put our financial house back in order because the sky would fall!" Well, with that approach our national debt has gone sky high. We spend more than we earn each year and are on a path towards bankruptcy. Unlike the government, we as individuals don't have the luxury of demanding more income when we spend too much so we are actually going to need to make some cuts. These cuts will allow you to pay off your debt and invest more. In the long run this will lead to more income and less debt. Wow, what a novel concept! Be prepared, the austerity riots are coming.

Fun Money

This may be one of the hardest areas to reduce your spending because fun money spending is often used to cope with the stresses of life. This is one area people often look to cut to help pay off debt or apply to other categories, but the Wealth Builder Lifestyle strongly advises against that. It's important to enjoy life and reward yourself. You work hard and make all kinds of sacrifices and deserve to be rewarded for your efforts.

The Wealth Builder Lifestyle's method of getting your fun money spending in balance is to set a budget and stick to it. Sounds easy, right? I'm joking! The way I recommend people successfully do this is by taking your fun money out in cash from every paycheck so that it's not mixed in with your other funds.

The reason for this is twofold. One, it's really easy to determine if you can afford to do something or not just by checking the balance of your pocket money. Two, by dealing with cash you are a lot more aware of how much things cost and how much you are spending. Psychologically speaking it is much less painful to swipe a credit or debit card to spend money than to deal in cash. This can lead to excessive small purchases, which can easily end up costing hundreds of dollars simply because it isn't easy to accurately track. When you use cash, you are going to feel it every time you break a hundred dollar bill (especially as your stack thins down).

So forget what you were spending before and replace that amount with the guideline amount in cash—no less, no more. You may feel some initial shock as you adjust, but the beauty of this method is that after the first time you run short and have to pass on doing something you really wanted to do, you will start paying much closer attention to how you spend. The next time you take your fun money allowance, you are going to value it more and in turn make sure that you are getting the maximum amount of enjoyment out of every dollar.

Another benefit people that use this method soon come to realize is that they look more creatively for ways to get the most enjoyment for the least amount of cost. We live in a great country filled with many great things to do that don't involve spending a lot of money. One option is to start exploring all your community has to offer, which can lead to increased physical activity, more awareness of your environment, and more quality time with family and friends.

This program is about building wealth consistently, but it has more to offer than just financial mastery. Opening up your mind and life to things that are not entirely money based can be extremely fulfilling and liberating. When you are not paying a price for every moment of enjoyment in your life, life gets a whole lot less expensive.

Discretionary Spending Cuts

What are your discretionary spending habits? List the typical daily expenses that you could eliminate. This could include eating out, purchasing unnecessary drinks or snacks, fueling up for errands you don't actually need to run, and so on. Put it all down. Don't worry, it may not be necessary for you to give all of these up, but nixing or limiting some of them may help you balance things out in the short run. After all, the goal of this program is to get you what you truly want without sacrificing your ability to build wealth.

Cutting your discretionary spending is often the easiest way to free up the money you need to get rebalanced. When it comes right down to it, a lot more of our money than we think is used in this way, and consequently, has no long-term value. What we spend in rent/housing expenses, phones, cable bills, utilities, etc. can often times be substantially reduced. The difference between the minimum we could spend on those items and what we choose to is what I call discretionary luxury spending.

People often tend to let the amount of money left in their bank account determine how much they spend on these unnecessary items. These purchases often originate from a need to fill time in our schedules and then quickly become bad habits that we start building our schedules around. Another common way we acquire these bad habits is in an attempt to deal with our emotional shortcomings. For example, going for that fancy coffee drink for comfort when things are stressful at work or maybe buying a six pack of beer each night to unwind.

Not only can these lifestyle habits be detrimental to building wealth, but they can often lead to poor health habits as well. It's no surprise that in the frantic, high-stress environment we live in these days people tend to turn to unhealthy solutions to cope. I'm not saying all of these things are bad by any means, but some may warrant a closer examination to see if they are truly serving you (as opposed to hurting you financially, physically, and emotionally). Drinking every night to cope with stress could lead to always being broke, which in turn creates more stress that will just make you want to drink even more. If you're at that point, you may want to rethink your plan.

Consistently investing even a small portion of what most people's discretionary spending is into an investment that gives a modest return, can lead to a substantial amount of wealth when it comes time to retire. Habits can lead you to being habitually poor or habitually rich. It's up to you to decide which type of habits you want to foster. It doesn't matter what you have done in the past, because new habits can be formed at any time. The key is to identify them, understand the future benefit or cost, and then instill new Wealth Builder habits.

Our goal is to be able to cut some of your discretionary spending to hopefully not only get you within the guidelines, but to also free up some extra money each month to pay down your high-interest, short-term debt. Keep that goal in mind as you grit your teeth about what you're considering giving up. Once you get your short-term debt paid down, you won't have those bills to pay anymore and you'll be in a much better financial position. I'm confident in saying that if you are carrying much credit card or other short-term debt, being free of that debt will be a liberating feeling that is well worth the sacrifice.

Use this form to enter any potential discretionary spending cuts you can think of. This is an exercise to evaluate as many options as you can come up with. You will make an actual list of the things you are going to cut later, so don't hold back now. Sometimes just running these numbers is an eye-opener to a lot of waste. This worksheet will also help you convert daily totals into a monthly total (which is what we will be using for your plan). For now, list all the items you could easily eliminate by simply making a different decision.

NOTES :

_____

_____

_____

_____

SPENDING ALIGNMENT

Multiply the amount of times a month you make this purchase by the cost to determine your monthly total.

Discretionary Spending Cuts		
Expense	Daily Expenditure	Monthly Total
1._____	$_____	$_____
2._____	$_____	$_____
3._____	$_____	$_____
4._____	$_____	$_____
5._____	$_____	$_____
6._____	$_____	$_____
7._____	$_____	$_____
8._____	$_____	$_____
9._____	$_____	$_____
10._____	$_____	$_____
11._____	$_____	$_____
12._____	$_____	$_____
13._____	$_____	$_____
14._____	$_____	$_____
15._____	$_____	$_____
16._____	$_____	$_____
17._____	$_____	$_____
18._____	$_____	$_____
19._____	$_____	$_____
20._____	$_____	$_____
Total Discretionary Cuts	$_____	$_____

Necessity Expenses

What is truly a "necessity?" In America, we are truly masters of making everything a necessity we just *have* to have. We can't fall behind, right? We need the latest technology, the fastest internet, thousands of television channels, the newest cars. The list goes on and on. Lo and behold, no matter how much we earn it just never seems to be enough. If you already spend less than the necessity principle guideline, you don't necessarily need to do this exercise but it might still be informative and give you some unexpected insight.

Be honest with yourself. Look at all the items you have that fall under the necessity expense category and come up with a list of things that you can and will cut to get within the guidelines. These items may not need to be totally eliminated, possibly just reduced. Work with your numbers until you get them inline or have cut everything that you possibly can. You don't have to give these things up permanently, but if you are not currently in a good wealth building situation, then cutting back or eliminating what you can for at least a while will be very beneficial. When you see how quickly you can start building wealth without these money leeches, you may never want them back.

In the following list, capture your necessity spending cuts including your action plan for making them and put them in ink. Some ideas might be to reduce your grocery expenses by shopping smarter or splurging less, changing your phone plan, getting rid of premium movie channels, unsubscribing from movie services, etc.

"There's nothing sexy about finance and numbers, but being wealthy will sure make you look and feel way more sexy!"

- Daniel Hartjoy

SPENDING ALIGNMENT

Enter the Necessity Spending items you will cut and your plan for making those cuts in the following form.

Necessity Spending Cuts		
Necessity Expense / Action Required		Monthly Total
1. _____ / _____		$ _____
2. _____ / _____		$ _____
3. _____ / _____		$ _____
4. _____ / _____		$ _____
5. _____ / _____		$ _____
6. _____ / _____		$ _____
7. _____ / _____		$ _____
8. _____ / _____		$ _____
9. _____ / _____		$ _____
10._____ / _____		$ _____
Total Necessity Spending Cuts		$ _____

Honestly, you may want to come back and chisel these expenses down more after you get further in and realize the true value of every dollar you spend versus invest. My sincerest hope is that when you've completed this program how you look at money will have totally changed. With any luck, you will be so tuned in to what it takes to be a successful wealth builder that you will feel pain when you see friends and family exercising the habits of the poor. Hopefully, that pain will motivate you to step up and help them turn their own financial lives around. Enter the total of any reduction in necessity expenses you came up with below.

Total Monthly Cash Available (from reducing necessity expenses)	$ _____

Personal Expenses

Personal expenses often have high emotional value. What does that mean? Well, many of these costs are for things like clothing, beauty products, higher education, and other items that make us feel better about ourselves. Eliminating these items just to save a dollar can lead to us being financially worth more but also to feeling less confident and unsure of ourselves. Be sure to maintain a good, honest balance between the two.

If you are not already under budget for this category, look closely at the personal expenses on your discretionary spending list. Thoughtfully go through these expenses to see how essential the things you spend money on are. See if there are some items that you could eliminate, or maybe just find a more affordable way to obtain the same result.

Use this form to capture any personal spending reductions you will make.

Personal Spending Cuts	
Personal Expense / Action Required	Monthly Total
1. _____ / _____	$ _____
2. _____ / _____	$ _____
3. _____ / _____	$ _____
4. _____ / _____	$ _____
5. _____ / _____	$ _____
6. _____ / _____	$ _____
7. _____ / _____	$ _____
8. _____ / _____	$ _____
9. _____ / _____	$ _____
10. _____ / _____	$ _____
Total Personal Spending Cuts	$ _____

SPENDING ALIGNMENT

Enter the total of any reduction in personal expenses you came up with below. Don't worry too much about getting things perfect as you can always move things around later to dial in your plan. It is a better strategy to be aggressive now and get everything on the table because then you can put some stuff back once your numbers begin to work.

Total Monthly Cash Available (from reducing personal expenses)	$ _____

NOTES :

_____

_____

_____

_____

_____

_____

_____

_____

_____

_____

_____

_____

_____

DEBT REDUCTION AND INVESTMENTS

We are going to be working on growing your income and wealth in many ways. Some of these methods can produce fast wealth gains while others can provide more of a steady cash flow (more commonly referred to as simply "income"). Regardless of how much your income grows, these core principles need to be a part of your habits and always respected.

I mention this now because we are slicing up what you already have like it is all you are ever going to have, which (naturally) can lead to discouragement. Rest assured, there are a lot of exciting opportunities coming your way. But, I don't believe in chasing pots of gold, which can lead to neglecting more sure-fire wealth building methods like practicing good financial habits. Living a lifestyle of chasing big gains (without heeding the wealth builder lifestyle principles) is a good way to end up broke later in life.

NOTES :

_____

_____

_____

_____

_____

_____

_____

PART TWO: TWELVE MONTH REBALANCE

Use the worksheets below to determine the modified program investment allocations you will be using during your rebalance period. During these first twelve months, we will morph the ultimate principles into achievable steps that move you towards your goal. This plan will allow you to free up money to put your short-term debt to rest using the upcoming debt-reduction strategy. Wait to enter your revised housing amount until after you complete the exercises in the upcoming housing section beginning on page 185.

Adjusted Spending (Twelve-Month Rebalance)					
Spending Items	Current Amount	Potential Reduction	Revised Amount	Program Guideline	New Net Difference
Housing (page 96 and 185+)	$_____	$_____	$_____	$_____	$_____
Necessity (page 96 and 117)	$_____	$_____	$_____	$_____	$_____
Personal (page 96 and 119)	$_____	$_____	$_____	$_____	$_____
Fun Money (page 96)	Guideline Amount		$_____	$_____	$_____
Security Cushion (page 110)	Monthly Amount		$_____	N/A	N/A
Total Spending and Security Cushion			$_____	$_____	$_____

Use the following form to easily subtract your total spending and cushion contributions from your monthly income. This will determine how much you can apply monthly towards debt reduction and investments.

Available Monthly Debt and Investment Funds (Twelve-Month Rebalance)	
Monthly Income (page 57)	$_____
	-
Spending and Security Cushion (above)	$_____
Total Monthly Balance	$_____

Debt Reduction Versus Investing

We will use some general weight principles to determine how much of your available money should go towards debt and how much should go towards investments. If you compare debt (with a 20% interest rate) to a possible investment (with a return of 10%), you'll find it obvious that you want to kill that debt first and as quickly as possible.

Going over the following guidelines is important. Feel free to move these numbers around a bit if you feel comfortable to get the best results. Just make sure you are still getting that debt knocked down quickly and that you continue investing. Redo the calculations every twelve months until your debt is gone.

NOTES :

PART TWO: TWELVE MONTH REBALANCE

Debt and Investment Calculator (Twelve-Month Rebalance)		
Total Debt (page 60)	**Total Income Balance After Expenses** (page 122)	**Months Required to Pay Off Debt**
$ _____	÷ $ _____	= _____

Option 1: If total months to pay off debt is less than 12, use the following formulas.

	Total Income Balance After Expenses	$ _____
Total Debt		-
$ _____	÷ 12 = **Monthly Debt Payment**	$ _____
		=
	Monthly Total to Invest	$ _____

Option 2: If total months to pay off debt is between 12 and 24, use the following formulas.

Total Income Balance After Expenses		Monthly Debt Payment
	× 0.70 =	$ _____
$ _____		**Monthly Total to Invest**
	× 0.30 =	$ _____

Option 3: If total months to pay off debt is over 24, use the following formulas.

Total Income Balance After Expenses		Monthly Debt Payment
	× 0.80 =	$ _____
$ _____		**Monthly Total To Invest**
	× 0.20 =	$ _____
Monthly Debt Reduction Payment		$ _____
Monthly Investment Contribution		$ _____

124

DEBT REDUCTION AND INVESTMENTS

Short-Term Debt Reduction

One of the best ways to grow wealth is to eliminate debt (which directly works against wealth building). There are actually ways to build wealth by leveraging debt, but that is not how most people use it. Most short-term debt carries too high of an interest rate to make it worth having, so wealth builders eliminate it. You will create a debt reduction hit list that will help you strategize the elimination of your debt in the quickest and most cost-effective way possible.

As I mentioned in the beginning of this program, there are four ways to live life. Most people live in a state of just sustaining themselves. If you are not able to get your finances inline with the principles for your income, you may need to temporarily move into a state of sacrificing. That may sound worse than sustaining, but trust me—it'll be well worth it. Temporarily, sacrificing can help catapult yourself from just financially sustaining to financially growing. That's a huge step up, so if you can get yourself into that position in only twelve months you will be feeling optimistic and living a new lifestyle of wealth creation.

Taking a slow, multi-year approach greatly increases the chances you will fail or just give up on changing your financial future. Sacrificing is painful, but from that pain can come positive, measurable results. The pain will keep you aware and focused on what you are doing, and the positive result will be proof that you are actually succeeding.

Hit List

The enemy deserves no mercy. Yep, time to go ahead and kill them. This enemy has been destroying lives for far too long. This is one death that requires no bloodshed. Nobody will feel bad about your actions, well—that is, except the bankers that you have been making rich all these years. Poor little banks! They will have to find a new sucker to suck dry of wealth.

Use this form to create a debt hit list targeted at super-charging your debt elimination. Combine your knowledge of the amount of income you have set aside for debt reduction with whichever of the following methods best suits your personal strengths to come up with a quick and effective debt-reduction plan.

There are three basic debt-reduction strategies commonly utilized: one will minimize the overall amount of interest you will pay; another specializes in rapidly freeing up financial resources and reducing the quantity of loans; and the third option is a blend of the two (which often works best for most).

Option One: Minimize Interest

Apply all your additional debt reduction money to the debt with the highest interest rate first. Then, continue on to the second highest, the third highest after that, and so on until they are all paid off. This is both the most cost effective and also the quickest way to pay off all your debts.

Option Two: Loan Elimination

Pay off your debts beginning with the smallest balance first. Then, move on to the second largest, the third largest, and so on until they are all paid off. This is neither the most cost effective nor quickest way, but often helps keep people optimistic by providing quicker individual debt eliminations. This method can also be beneficial if you are very short on money each month as it will reduce your minimum expenses quicker by eliminating the payments from those smaller loans.

Option Three: Wealth Builder Lifestyle

By taking a mix of the above two options, this method can help free up cash *and* eliminate the number of bills you have to pay each month. The benefits of this are that you get a rapid sense of accomplishment and an added safety net (because of the extra available cash) while still keeping the overall interest paid to a minimum. To use this method, use Option Two for up to six months to knock out some small loans quickly before transitioning on to Option One to avoid paying excessive interest. The following worksheet shows an example hit list based on Option Three: Wealth Builder Method.

Hit List (Hit Amount: *$90*)						
Creditor	Loan Balance	Minimum Payment	Hit List Payment	Hit Start Date	Payoff Date	A P R
Example Loan 1	*~~$600~~*	*$60*	*$150*	*1/1/2013*	*4/1/2013*	*12%*
Example Loan 2	*~~$1,250~~*	*$75*	*$225*	*5/1/2013*	*9/1/2013*	*19%*
Example Loan 3	*~~$500~~*	*$35*	*$260*	*10/1/2013*	*10/1/2013*	*6%*
Example Loan 4	*$5,000*	*$250*	*$510*	*11/1/2013*	*3/1/2014*	*12%*
Initial Loan Total	**$7,350**		**Yearend Balance**		**$1,530**	

You will find your own worksheet to fill in on the next page. To determine your total Hit Amount, subtract your Minimum Payment Combined Total (from the Current Short-Term Debts form on page 60) from your Monthly Debt Reduction Payment (from the Debt and Investment Calculator on page 124). Continue by entering your current loans, balances, APRs, and minimum payments (and list them in the order you want to pay them off in, which should be based on the method you chose).

To determine the Hit List Payment amount, add the Hit Amount to the Minimum Payment for your first target. Figure out how many months it will take at that rate to pay it off and from that determine the Payoff Date. The Hit Start Date will be the following month after you successfully pay off a debt. The hit start and payoff dates do not need to be exact. To calculate the dates, just assume that 100% of each payment will be applied to the debt's principal and round up on the last month (to account for some interest expenses).

Now that the first loan is paid off, take that minimum payment and the Hit List Payment and add it the Minimum Payment for your next target debt. Continue down the list until you reach your last debt. You will have to do a little math to determine your yearend balance, especially if you have a large amount of debt or limited income to apply to debt reduction. If you need additional space, make some extra copies of this form and carry over your totals.

Hit List (Hit Amount $ _____)						
Creditor	Loan Balance	Minimum Payment	Hit List Payment	Hit Start Date	Payoff Date	APR
_____	$_____	$_____	$_____	_____	_____	___
_____	$_____	$_____	$_____	_____	_____	___
_____	$_____	$_____	$_____	_____	_____	___
_____	$_____	$_____	$_____	_____	_____	___
_____	$_____	$_____	$_____	_____	_____	___
_____	$_____	$_____	$_____	_____	_____	___
_____	$_____	$_____	$_____	_____	_____	___
_____	$_____	$_____	$_____	_____	_____	___
_____	$_____	$_____	$_____	_____	_____	___
_____	$_____	$_____	$_____	_____	_____	___
_____	$_____	$_____	$_____	_____	_____	___
Initial Loan Total $_____			Yearend Balance		$_____	

It's easy to get excited about finally getting started on saving and investing. Everyone's enthusiastic about seeing positive asset growth! Unfortunately, forgetting about debt reduction can actually lead to going backwards financially, especially if your debts have higher interest rates than the anticipated returns on your investments.

Building wealth is about building good financial habits and sticking to them. I recommend you start building and reinforcing all your new financial habits right away while they are still fresh in your mind. You don't have to wait until you get all your short-term debt paid off to begin saving and investing. Take at least a small amount out of every paycheck to save and invest it. By doing this you will be establishing a habit of saving and investing a portion of all your income.

Each time you pay off a short-term loan, ratchet up your savings and investments just a bit. Maybe set aside $5 extra from each paycheck and roll the rest into your next hit list debt. This will help your investments start to accelerate and show a little more fruit while reinforcing good financial habits.

Do not incur more debt!

I know you may be feeling card-swiping withdrawals—you *have* been being good, right? Don't give in to the urges! Keep one or two credit cards handy for emergencies **only**. (And keep in mind, retail therapy is not an emergency!)

Debt, Spending, and Investment Summary

Enter the results from your previous calculations into the following form which you will use as a reference for the next twelve months on how, where, and when to allocate your income. It's important to setup your investment contributions to come directly out of your paycheck the day you receive it, if at all possible. On payday, immediately withdraw enough cash to cover your fun money and personal expenses so you are not tempted to use your debit or credit cards to pay for them. Setup automatic payments for your bills if possible so you can just make your deposit and forget about it.

The more isolated and separate you can keep these items, the better success you will have. Once everything is set up, you should rarely need to access your debit cards, credit cards, or checking accounts because your small, frequent transactions will be done in cash. When you're finished, make a copy of the following sheet so you can keep it handy.

PART TWO: TWELVE MONTH REBALANCE

Rebalance Summary	
Spending I will reduce (or cut entirely) for the next twelve months:	
Necessity Spending	**Personal Spending**
1. _____	1. _____
2. _____	2. _____
3. _____	3. _____
4. _____	4. _____
5. _____	5. _____
6. _____	6. _____
7. _____	7. _____
8. _____	8. _____
9. _____	9. _____
10. _____	10. _____

Expense Budgets		
Item	**Location to Keep Funds**	**Amount**
Housing Expenses (page 122)	Checking Account	$_____
Necessity Expenses (page 122)	Checking Account	$_____
Personal Expenses (page 122)	Cash	$_____
Fun Money (page 122)	Cash	$_____

Security Cushion		
Security Cushion (page 122)	Savings or Liquid Asset	$_____

Short-Term Debt Reduction		
Item	**When to Pay**	**Amount**
Debt Reduction (page 124)	Immediately Each Paycheck	$_____

Investments		
Monthly Investments (page 124)	Immediately Each Paycheck	$_____
Total of All Expenses (should not exceed income)		$_____

CAREER FAST-TRACKING

Thought you were in deep before? Well, now we are going to raise the bar. Better to aim higher than the mark, than to aim for the mark and come up short. If you come up a little short on the high target, you may still clear the bar. If you come up a little short when aiming to just barely clear the bar, you'll miss.

Ultimate Income Requirement

What is your current income? _____

Does this adequately meet your financial needs? Yes _____ No _____

How many hours a week does your career consume? (Travel, work at home, etc.) _____

Can you currently afford all the material goods and services you desire? Yes_____ No_____

What are the five most significant things (if any) you are lacking due to your current level of income?

1. _____
2. _____
3. _____
4. _____
5. _____

PART TWO: TWELVE MONTH REBALANCE

Although we will always talk of keeping your debt down and watching your spending, we've no intention for you to have to live like a pauper all your life. Just the opposite, in fact. The main objective is to ensure you keep making progress on wealth building. You can't afford to sacrifice financial growth for momentary enjoyment. Most people put fun "in the moment" before wealth building and thus never get around to actually building the wealth. This doesn't work out in the long run and has harsh consequences that nobody wants.

As your income grows, all your categories increase. Your wealth building will accelerate, and your fun money will increase with it. We all want that. Heck, it's fun, right? Just don't commit financial suicide by using the debt trap to live an artificially wealthy life. Earn and live a *real* life of wealth.

This exercise is to determine how much income you would need to live your ultimate lifestyle. Go ahead and find out how much you would need to earn to afford everything you really want. I advise you to be liberal here and just put it all out there. Most people hold themselves back financially because of unfounded personal beliefs about how much money they could earn, ultimately settling for far less than they are capable of achieving.

I'm speaking as a former "self-limiter." When my personal beliefs were shattered by someone who pushed me to do what I perceived as unthinkable, I was amazed at how much I could earn and how quickly I could change my income. It was a profound life-changing and eye-opening experience, one I hope I can help you create.

"Expecting to be wealthy without a clear picture of what it takes for you to be wealthy and a clear plan to get you there will keep you right where you are."

- Daniel Hartjoy

CAREER FAST-TRACKING
My Ultimate Lifestyle

To complete the My Ultimate Lifestyle worksheet, create a list of your ultimate desires and calculate just how much they would cost. It will be a big help if you have a calculator and the internet available so you can determine their actual cost and compute the necessary loan payments. It's not necessary to get overly detailed in adding the cents—just round numbers will do. Don't worry about how big the numbers get, just be honest about what you really want.

Be sure you are thoroughly thinking through the things you actually want in your life. Remember, this isn't a sweepstakes where you just throw anything you can think of into the cart regardless of whether you really want it or not. You will still have to pay for this stuff. If you don't want it, don't put it down. It's foolish to buy it just because you can.

NOTES :

_____

_____

_____

_____

_____

_____

_____

_____

_____

_____

PART TWO: TWELVE MONTH REBALANCE

Work through the following form to determine the monthly expenses for your dream lifestyle.

My Ultimate Lifestyle					
Item	Total Costs	Monthly Payments	Monthly Insurance	Monthly Expenses	Monthly Totals
Home	$_____	$_____	$_____	$_____	$_____
Auto 1	$_____	$_____	$_____	$_____	$_____
Auto 2	$_____	$_____	$_____	$_____	$_____
Education	$_____	$_____	$_____	$_____	$_____
Boat	$_____	$_____	$_____	$_____	$_____
Motorcycle	$_____	$_____	$_____	$_____	$_____
RV	$_____	$_____	$_____	$_____	$_____
Travel	$_____	$_____	$_____	$_____	$_____
Vacations	$_____	$_____	$_____	$_____	$_____
Other	$_____	$_____	$_____	$_____	$_____
Other	$_____	$_____	$_____	$_____	$_____
Other	$_____	$_____	$_____	$_____	$_____
Grand Totals	$_____	$_____	$_____	$_____	$_____

So, what was your total? Was it higher or lower than you actually thought it would be? Hopefully you enjoyed just thinking about the fun you could have with all that stuff.

We are very fortunate to have so many opportunities available to us. Having big dreams and inspirational goals can be very motivating. Just be sure to keep positive energy flowing in your life by maintaining a happy atmosphere and an optimistic outlook, then money (and all the other things you want) will come much easier. Some things can't be forced. You just need to be focused, consistent, and constantly moving in the right direction. As long as you're doing that, you need only let the rest happen!

Enter the total monthly cost of your dream lifestyle below:

Ultimate Lifestyle Monthly Cost	$ _____

Base Income Goal

As you setup your life to build wealth and enjoy the lifestyle you want, you need to know what kind of income you're actually going to need. If you have, for example, a $150,000 a year dream lifestyle and are in a career that has a top earning potential of $50,000, you have a big problem. This is a common predicament for people who pick their career before determining the cost of their desired lifestyle.

Amazingly, most people I have met have either chosen their careers first or just fallen into them by chance. This predetermines the financial limitations of their lifestyle. They then work to live within their means, which (as so many know) is often unfulfilling and rarely successfully accomplished. So saving and investing are usually forgone for living a better lifestyle in the present.

Use this form to get a ballpark calculation of the annual income you would need to live your ultimate lifestyle. Don't worry if it seems out of your reach. When you learn to live the Wealth Builder Lifestyle, money will be easier for you to obtain. This is precisely why the rich keep getting richer. Once you figure it out, wealth will become increasingly accessible and you will find that there are many ways to grow your prosperity outside of just your career.

Dream Lifestyle Income Calculator		
Dream Lifestyle Monthly Cost	(accounts for your taxes and investments)	Annual Income Need
$ _____	× 2 = $ _____	× 12 = $ _____
This calculation leaves 50% of your income to cover your taxes, savings, and investment funds.		

So, how does your current income match up with your dream lifestyle cost? Does your current career have the potential to ever meet your dream lifestyle income requirement?

The next step in this program is going to take a serious look at your career in a number of ways. By doing so you can determine if there are changes that can be made within your current career that would allow you to increase your income. This may be possible by acquiring additional certifications or degrees, changing your place of employment, or maybe even by pursuing a promotion in a new way.

Very few people end up where they want to go without first determining where it is they want to go. You now know what size of income you ultimately want, which is the first step in achieving your dream lifestyle. I see it frequently: people just settle in and accept their income, like they're at the end and any increase is out of their hands now. They just hope and wait for that little raise that will hopefully keep up with the cost of inflation.

Those aren't real increases in income. They're just keeping you from sinking, so it won't get too painful and cause you to quit. Each year the cost of everything increases about 3-4%, so a 3-4% raise is essential just to keep you from falling backwards. Contrary to what you'd think this little raise would mean, it has not improved your financial situation in the least.

Job Commoditization

As the ideas and products we once saw as new become known, their prices and the careers related to them go through a process I call "job commoditization." As with any commodity, over time we discover and incorporate every imaginable efficiency into the creation process and develop training programs to create an abundance of workers specializing in the specific skill sets required. As we move towards and reach that point, the item's unit cost goes down and pay rates stabilize (and often times even fall).

Take, for instance, the web design industry. When this industry first exploded, we had a huge demand for its services and few workers with the necessary skills (since it was a new technology). The people that had those skills were very valuable and in high demand. Over time we have trained an abundance of people to perform those roles while simultaneously improving the related technology used to create websites. What used to take serious coding knowledge (which few knew how to do) now has literally become "drag-and-drop" simple,

136

requiring little to no coding at all. Therefore, while many spent money and time getting the education necessary to acquire those seemingly well-paid jobs, the pay started coming down due to the technological advances in web-building tools and the increased supply of qualified workers. Now there is an over abundance of people who can build websites, and it's only natural that the pay reflects it. Today, twelve-year-old kids can build high quality websites and skilled people are willing to do it for $10 an hour. Do you really want to compete with them to make a living?

This is the unfortunate state of the world we are living in. Things are changing at the speed of light, and if you're not changing with it, you will get left behind. This is why it's so important to be on top of your finances and have a solid plan.

While good pay becomes more elusive, the rich and big businesses prosper by using strategies that make their money grow under such conditions. The web design industry may no longer be particularly lucrative, but there are plenty of others that still are. One such place is capital-intensive businesses. They require a lot of money to get into, and therefore few (pretty much only the rich) can afford to get into them. This allows the wealthy some prime, exclusive income opportunities.

It used to be that a good idea and some hard work was all it took to get ahead. Today, unfortunately, that's rarely good enough. In a world where information travels fast and things can go viral overnight, a little leak of your idea and a hungry business or individual can throw untold resources at your idea and be the first to bring it to market. This can put you in a position of playing catch-up or cause you to lose out altogether. I'm not telling you these things to discourage you, I'm telling you so you understand the dynamics of today's economy and have a chance to compete.

Today even holding something like a patent or copyright is often times not enough to protect yourself. People are willing to steal ideas and violate these perceived securities, so often it's up to you to sue them to recover any damages. Unfortunately, an endeavor like that can cost a fortune and if you don't have the money to fight them you are at a huge disadvantage.

Exporting of Jobs

You hear a lot of talk about overseas manufacturing and bringing those jobs back to the US. As good as that sounds, based on what I have just told you those jobs are often times no longer what they used to be.

It is impossible for the US to compete with overseas labor. Think about this: it used to be we could charge more for American-made products because the quality was superior to places like China and other foreign countries. But those days are long gone. Remember what I said about information and keeping secrets? China (as well as other countries) is now as good (or better) than us at manufacturing. They have seen the opportunity, gone in after the necessary information, tools, and skills, and have effectively conquered these challenges with a vengeance. It's a very competitive market out there and to be competitive we would have to be working at wages so cheap we wouldn't be able to afford to live in the US.

Take for example the iPhone and iPad. They are solid proof that some of the highest quality and most technologically advanced products are now successfully being made in China, a country once laughed at for producing low-quality junk. Do we want the high-tech jobs of manufacturing those products back? Maybe, but a lot of the high-tech work is done by high-tech machines, reducing the labor portion to a low-paying, virtually unskilled job.

If you want to succeed today, you really need to retrain your mind and sharpen your tools. Two things these international countries still struggle with are ideas and creativity. Those companies need to know *what* to make, so they turn to those who have the next great idea that will create the new markets and opportunities.

I think we are actually in a time when the thinkers and creative types are going to be able to create a lot of wealth because our global economy is seeking those new ideas passionately. We need something to reinvigorate our economic engines, and it's not likely to come in the known ideas of the past. We have major environmental issues that are not going to allow us to adequately grow our wealth and economies based on the consumption-based model that brought us this far.

As countries like China grow and become more like the US they will look to have the same type of material goods and lifestyles as the average American. This approach will create an environmental disaster that will have serious consequences. If China copies America's material-driven lifestyle, pollution will continue to grow out of control due to the fact that they have over four times the population of the US. I'm not talking about global warming (a political hotbed already), I'm talking about polluted water sources, airborne particles, toxic chemical exposures, and so on. The things I'm talking about are not even debatable—I have seen them first hand and have no doubts about their existence or impact.

So why is this a good time for people to build wealth? What does all that mean? Because where we spend dollars will be on the move, therefore many opportunities for new businesses and careers will be created. The key word here is **new**. When something first comes online, the pay and opportunities are often far better.

I think we are going to see a transition away from so many material goods towards things that have less of an environmental impact. This may come in the form of more live entertainment, more education and training in new skills (beyond typical K-12 and college classes), more unique services, and numerous other additions. Some of the expansion areas I'm talking about have yet to be discovered.

The Rich and Poor Gap

So how do we keep from ending up in dead-end, low-paying jobs with lots of competition? For one, you need to be proactive and keep your eyes open to what is going on in the world around you. Don't let yourself get distracted by the news, media, and politicians rousing anger about the rich and poor gap. It is there and growing—which is one of the primary reasons why I created this program—but getting upset or distressed about it is not going to help change your fate. Holding your breath and waiting for the Democrats or Republicans to fix it will get you nowhere, and that time spent waiting will put you even further behind.

I think any attempts by politicians to create a solution will likely only make the problems worse. We have within us everything needed to create a solution *individually*. The actions of a few creating new laws are not going to be able to ensure millions get inspired to think and act for themselves proactively and creatively.

What built the US and global economy at large is the freedom, creativity and drive of individuals. As long as you are willing to wait for a solution, the rich will continue to get richer and you will stay where you are or fall behind. Take the information in this program and put it to work. This is the same information the rich people use to get rich. They have already figured it out and use it themselves. Once your wealth starts to grow, every future dollar you earn gets easier and comes quicker. That is why they continue to get richer, even in down times.

A lot of rich people didn't start out rich. The beauty is that you currently have many of the opportunities they have. Sure, you may be excluded from some because you are not yet financially well off, but as of today, you still have the right and opportunity to get wealthy.

If you are a supporter of taxing the rich in some attempt to get their money passed down to you, take these few things into consideration. First of all, if you do take action and start to build your own wealth, you will run into the taxes you so desired, which will ultimately make it harder for you to get ahead. Secondly, the money will always leave those that don't understand it and return to those who do. So, the resulting outcome will be that this new obstacle will only make it harder for you while the rich will work around it and continue to successfully grow their wealth.

One of the big tax targets is investment income. Why? Because it would take money primarily from the wealthy, since most low-income and poorer people don't invest. Investing is one of the best financial tools available in our country. You don't have to be rich to invest, and it's a key tool for building wealth. That's why this tax would hurt the poor and less fortunate the most. Maybe not initially, but surely over the long term. A far better solution to such tax changes would be to teach the poor about investing and get them into wealth building through it.

Once this new tax is in place, it will limit the ability for everyone to build wealth through investing. Sure, the rich people have more money to lose (if you look at the dollar amount, since they have much more money invested), but the real loss will come to those with the least, since it will slow their growth potential. And don't they need the fastest growth possible? Don't look at the wealthy and try to create obstacles that will stop them from building wealth. Copy them, do the same things they do and you too will get the same results.

Career Fast-Tracking

We know it's more important than ever to make sure we maximize our income and do the right things with our money, so how do we do it?

Through positive role models and life experiences, I've been blessed to have my eyes opened to different "actualities." I say "actualities" here because I believe reality is totally changeable. If so, then there is essentially no such thing as definite reality—only what you believe reality will be. My understanding of what reality is has been shattered so many times and allowed a much better "actuality" that I think it is important to keep things in perspective.

I was able to greatly accelerate my career and income because I challenged what most people would accept as reality. I hope I can impact you in a way that will help you break down the walls created by your own beliefs. I believe we limit ourselves with what we believe to be the reality of what our future holds. When you challenge your beliefs you open up your life to endless opportunities—opportunities to try and do the things you never would have thought possible.

So if there is no such thing as reality (and consequently there is only the illusion of reality), why can't we just change it in any way we want? Well, who said you can't? If you believe something about your future is possible, your chances of it being true go up dramatically. If you believe, "I will never be able to earn over $50,000 a year," (or whatever your target number is) there is a good chance you are right. Regardless of whether you actually could or not, because you already accepted that defeat as your reality, victory is no longer considered as a possibility. On the other hand, if you believe that within the next five years you will make $100,000 (and you take action toward that goal) the chances you will blow past that $50,000 mark certainly shoot way up. Believe me, once you have gone from $50,000 to $100,000 then $100,000 to $150,000 is even easier.

All right, so now you probably think I'm talking nonsense. I get that. So, let's talk about how this craziness can go from virtual reality to actuality.

Goal

You need to start with an income goal. You should have previously determined what your ideal income goal would be as well as what your current income needs are (enough to cover your essential investments and expenses). If you are not yet comfortable aiming for your ideal income, select something you are comfortable with that will exceed your current income needs by an amount that will excite and motivate you.

You can *absolutely* shoot for your ideal income right out of the gate, if you want. I'm a proponent of going large and aiming as high as you want. For some people, that approach may be inconceivable this early in their financial lifestyle transformation. For them, aiming too high too soon could lead to a feeling of being overwhelmed and result in discouragement, thus increasing the likelihood of falling out of the program. You will have to make the call based on your own personality type and take the approach that's right for you.

Regardless of where you set your goal today, I want you to certainly keep your thoughts looking out beyond that goal. For example, even if your compromise was a $100,000 income I don't recommend going into a specialized field that has a $100,000 cap with no potential for growth towards your ideal goal.

You can't afford to think in the short term, especially considering how drastically things can change and that our most well-constructed plans can easily become obsolete before we ever reach our goals. I frequently run into people who got a lot of specialized training and then realized they don't even like the field they are in, or outsourcing or other changes eliminated the demand. At that point, they realize they have spent a bunch of money and time getting prepared for something that is no longer of value to them.

By thinking beyond your initial goal you can try to tailor your training, skills, achievements, and experiences to be diverse and applicable in multiple fields, reducing your chances of disappointment or a major setback.

Personal Fit

This is probably one of the most overlooked, yet absolutely essential items to fully maximizing your career and getting fulfillment out of it. You are going to dedicate a lot of your life (and some of your best years) to your career, so you want to make sure you will enjoy it. Work does not have to be about sacrificing.

If you really want to excel in any career or business, do something you love and have passion for. Passion comes a lot easier when you love what you do. This is a surefire way to make sure you can happily put your heart and soul into your career, which in the end will yield the maximum amount of fruits for your labor. If you want a happy and fulfilling life, go back and read the last two sentences again as it is a major key to that end. Today, our society really focuses on and revolves around money, but despite its essentiality, if you don't love what you're doing, no amount of money will bring you happiness doing it.

Time—not money—is the currency of life. You can make more money, but you can't make more time. None of us know how much time we have left, so we had better make the most of it and enjoy every moment to the best of our abilities. Yes, money can buy you freedom so you can do the things you want with your free time, but most people fall into a vicious trap in their pursuit of currency. When they earn more, they then spend more. They continually raise the cost of their lifestyle or desires so they must earn even *more* to afford that freedom. After living their life in that cycle, they inevitably look back and realize that they gave up all their time chasing a goal they could never achieve based on their pattern of constantly raising the bar.

How many people do you know that have made their share of money and are now reveling in the time and life they ultimately wanted? I would guess very few. I work in a field that I absolutely love and would do for free, so every moment I spend working is a great and fulfilling moment of my life. That's what makes going to work easy, and it also makes me committed to doing my job to the very best of my abilities.

Seven Things You Absolutely Need

That wasn't always my life, and getting here wasn't easy. I had to walk away from an industry that I had mastered and put virtually every penny I had accumulated on the line to get to where I am today. That was a huge risk, one I would have liked to have avoided. Unfortunately, I was never taught what I actually needed out of a career to be fulfilled and happy. Otherwise, I would have pursued a different direction right from the start.

That being said, when I found my true calling my heart was in it, so I pursued the skills and knowledge I needed with a passion. I never considered failure. I aimed high with the belief that I could (and would) achieve my dreams. During what should have been the hardest times—during which I was financially on the edge, overwhelmed with learning, working my tail off, and in a position where I could have easily quit and walked away—the thought never crossed my mind. I was doing what I loved and was fulfilled emotionally by each new step closer to my goal, which just made me stronger. Although I didn't have the money yet, I also didn't have the need for all the things I once thought I did to be happy and fulfilled.

So make sure your career or business pursuits involve something you really have a passion for. Below we will revisit the Seven Human Needs and how they absolutely affect the fulfillment you will get out of your career.

Sustenance

I don't believe in working just to sustain myself. When you get skills or training, you want to make sure you will always be broadly marketable. Make sure you will always be in demand to a level where you are certain you can sustain your base living and lifestyle.

Connection

Will this direction put you in a group of like-minded people that you have things in common with that can positively complement and enhance your life? Will you be working with people that are of a caliber that you would want to build a relationship with and spend time around? This is important because most people spend at least a third of each weekday at work, so this will be a key source of building friends and relationships (which are essential components of a good life).

Security

Will this career give you financial security and peace of mind? Will it allow you to grow financially for a long period of time? Is it stable? And if not, will the skills and experience you obtain allow you to easily cross over to another career path while still maintaining your financial security?

Growth

Will you continue to grow and develop new skills? Does the industry have room for growth and innovation that will keep it relevant? Are you going to be able to achieve new goals and continually expand yourself through your efforts?

Significance

Will this path give you a feeling of significance? Will this job be rewarding in a way that makes you feel good about what you are doing? Doing something that adds value to other peoples' lives often leads to a feeling of significance. Earning a good income and having the respect of your peers can also lead to feeling significant. If you don't feel good about what you are doing or you're doing something that you're not appreciated for you will likely feel insignificant and have very little motivation to perform well.

Esteem

Will this career and work environment give you confidence and a sense of pride? Will it allow you to feel good about what you are doing and have done? Will you be able to excel and be looked upon as a great contributing asset?

Inner Peace

Ultimately inner peace is what we all need and strive for. It's what motivates us to pursue the fulfillment of all our needs. Will your career choice broadly serve your six other needs as well as give you the potential to meet your need for inner peace and fulfillment?

   If your career can fulfill the general needs we all have, you are far more likely to feel fulfilled and enjoy what you are doing. This can help take the negative aspect of "work" out of earning an income and replace it with something far more pleasurable.

Overpriced Education

When evaluating any career advancement, it is important to analyze the expense of that perceived advancement. When an economy is struggling, people will often spend a lot of money and energy doing retraining and trying to advance their education. This is a great idea conceptually, but I have seen too many go at it blindly without figuring in the cost to make sure it will actually make sense in the long run.

It's important to take into consideration not only the cost of the training or schooling but also your lost income earning potential for that period of time. If well thought-out and properly executed, this can really increase your working years' income potential. If done wrong, it can put you in debt and become a waste of time. These days, this risk can be excessively high in many fields as job commoditization takes effect.

A lot of people think that doctors are rich and overpaid without ever taking into consideration all the time and cost they had to invest to get to the point of earning that type of income. They will likely have lost ten or more income-earning years and been unable to invest during that time. Not only that, but they've probably taken on substantial debt and will have the interest on that debt working against them for years beyond when they start earning. We typically will dedicate forty or more years to earning a living and building our retirements, while they will have only about thirty to do so.

Looking at the big picture, doctors very well may earn a high income once working. But their total life earnings need to be compared to accurately determine the true value of that career. A quick analysis would be to take the value of their 30 years of income, subtract their education and training expenses, and then divide it by 40. Even this is not a totally fair way to look at it since they have likely put off long-term investments for ten or more years longer than the rest of us. This means their investments will not benefit from ten of the most powerful years of compound interest growth.

Make sure you look at the bigger picture when making your career training and education decisions so you can make sure that over the long run they make as much sense as they initially appear to. If you lose five years of income earning just for training, you had better make sure the increase in pay is virtually assured and will offset your education expenses, lost income, and bypassed investment opportunities by a decent margin. If the advancement opportunity you are looking into doesn't meet that criteria, you may want to think it through a little further and possibly take another path all together.

Education

I'm not sold on education, education, and more education in the same way many are. I think getting an education for a career makes sense, but only when it is specifically applicable and not as a general rule. I see more and more people coming out of college with no job prospects. They didn't have a set direction and didn't get any specific training that qualified them for anything in particular. They then enter the working world with a lot of debt, only to be disappointed by the lack of good job opportunities. That was not what they were sold on going in, and now after a lot of hard work and commitment they feel ripped off—and rightfully so.

I understand most people coming out of high school may not know exactly which direction they want to go with their careers. I think one of the most substantial benefits that an employer gets from someone with a four-year degree is that they can easily see a level of commitment to pursue a better life in that worker. This is not to be underestimated by any means, and I think it's highly desirable, but a trait like that needs to be complimented with a bigger plan and an intention of getting somewhere specific (or an attainment of skills that are broadly marketable and sought after).

148

I said to keep your marketability broad, so when I say shoot for something specific, I'm not saying abandon diverse and marketable skills. You want to achieve both. Today, a lot of people are going to vocational schools or getting specific training for certain careers. I think this route also needs to be well thought out if it's going to be successful. You are investing time, energy, and money into very specific training that may only be usable in one profession or career. This can often power you up and make you valuable to that specific industry, but also make you very vulnerable to job commoditization.

Depending on your career choice and goals, that may not be an issue. If the money is suitable to your lifestyle and it fulfills your needs, then it could be a perfect course and shortcut over the typical four-year degree. The downside is (and the reason this can lead to job commoditization) that because your skills are not necessarily valuable outside that specific market, your employer undoubtedly also knows that your options are limited. Consequently, this can allow them to keep your pay down without a high risk of losing you as their wealth building asset.

Make Good Career Decisions

We live in very fast moving and changing times. The paths of yesterday aren't necessarily going to fit within today's job market and societal demands. This is where it's critical for you to think about what you really want out of life financially, and, (even more importantly) your career environment and opportunities. There is no correct blanket decision that will work universally to lead someone towards a fulfilling, financially-rewarding, and prosperous career. We each have our own unique traits, desires, and talents, so we need to take the information available and personally decide our best course of action.

Financially

You need to consider the lost earning and investment cost when you pursue your education and make sure the sacrifice is worth the reward.

This really needs to be done thoughtfully, looking way down the road. It's certainly a lot easier to get a higher education when you are young and unburdened, so don't skip it for the quick buck. Just make sure your big-picture plans make financial sense.

College

I think this is a great asset for attracting companies and giving them the confidence that if they invest their time and money into training you to fulfill their needs that you will stick around. This comfort can open the door to a lot of opportunities even without any trade-specific training. As a business owner, I often look at how secure my investment in an employee will be down the road. I don't want to waste my time training someone only to have to retrain the next person when they move on or flake out. Personally, I think everyone has potential and can be trained to do almost anything regardless of their educational background or degrees. But I am far less likely to invest in someone who does not have a track record of commitment and willingness to invest in themselves. A degree is proof that you have committed to making your life better, which is an admirable and a desirable characteristic.

Trade-Specific Training

If you know where you want to go and will be content in one specific industry or area of expertise, this can fast-track you towards higher earnings by developing marketable skills. The risks to consider here are possibly outgrowing your career and potential changes in the industry you pick, which may put you at a disadvantage later in life. For many this could quickly lead to a substantial increase in pay and job security compared to what they currently have, especially if they have no other professional training.

Personal Skill Development

I think this is something everyone should work on regardless of where they are currently or where they want to go. A college degree may be able to open a door for you, but well-rounded personal skills will be what propel you rapidly to the top in anything you do. I think that this is the future of career development and marketability. In a society that is moving so fast, is so complex, and is changing by the minute, learning what you needed to know yesterday will be of little value. And colleges can't teach you what you will need to know tomorrow, because (obviously) it's not yet known.

The best way to prepare for that and to be of great value is to become well rounded. Some people are naturally well rounded because they picked up their skills from their environment or upbringing, while others have moderate to substantial weaknesses or holes in their personal skills. These holes can all be filled in, and there are a lot of specific courses available to focus on virtually any weakness in order to eliminate it. Not all of these skills can or will go on your resume, but they will certainly show up in your interview, your work performance, and overall ability to add value to a team.

The types of applicable personal skills are numerous: selling, managing, negotiating, communicating, team building, and so on. These skills are not universally taught to us along the way, but many of these key aspects will be mastered by and present in the most successful in life. For example, when I talk about selling, that doesn't just relate to a sales career. To get ahead in life, you will frequently have to successfully sell yourself. Take for instance getting hired. You need to be able to sell yourself and show a potential employer the value you will add to their company. You will have to successfully sell your abilities long before you will ever get the chance to demonstrate them. If you want a raise and it's not being offered, you'd better understand how things work and how to tactfully sell the fact that you deserve a raise.

Summary

In general, I don't think you can solely apply any one particular approach in order to succeed. If you truly want to be successful, your specific situation will likely require a blended approach. If you are in college and know a specific industry you want to go into, you may want to get a certification or take a trade school course simultaneously. That way when you hit the job market you are seriously prepared. This may require a little more thought and work on your behalf, but it could catapult your career ahead by years, making you more marketable and worthy of a higher starting salary.

It's never too late. These things apply regardless of your age, race, education, and experience. The later in life (or the more disadvantaged) you are the more critical it will be that you give these things adequate consideration and properly implement these concepts. Not only is it never too late, but **now is always the best time** to make your plans. Waiting is never a good idea.

Foresight and Anticipation

Regardless of whether you choose to grow your income via a business or by further career development, it is essential that you make every effort to foresee what is coming in the future. This is a skill too few have (or at least utilize). There are no crystal balls that I know of for foreseeing the future, but that is always where the money is.

Our world and economy are changing at the speed of light. Never in our history have things changed so fast. This creates many challenges for those that just want to relax and not have to think or strategize too much. It also creates continual opportunities for those who will step up, get informed, and think ahead. This puts the complacent non-thinker at a huge disadvantage and at the mercy of those who are embracing this new way of life.

Could you imagine taking an iPad back and showing it to a caveman? They would look at you like a two-headed snake and probably strike you down with a club. For one, they have never seen anything like that before. Two, they wouldn't have a clue how to use it. Things have changed a lot since then, and if you saw a caveman today you would probably grab a video of him and run off screaming looking for help. By the time you found help, you would have probably already posted that video on YouTube and Facebook, acquiring hundreds of thousands of likes and a viral campaign.

Today, things become obsolete not in hundreds of years but often in just a few. Sometimes, they are lucky to make it even a year. Remember huge cell phones, pagers, dial-up internet lines, and tube televisions? These were all great, revolutionary products that people made fortunes on, but their time has passed. And things are moving even faster now! Innovations like MySpace pop up, appear promising, and then boom—Facebook shows up and begins dominating. Before you know it, MySpace is virtually gone and you vaguely remember it ever existed (let alone care).

It seems pointless now to try to get into that industry. If things move so fast, why should we invest the time and energy only to have what we are building become obsolete shortly after we get it to market? That is where the opportunity lies. You need to be building (or a part of the building of) the next best thing that nobody has heard of yet. Unlike in the past when businesses remained for a long time and owners would continually focus on perfecting what they were doing, now consumers are ready for the next thing before they figure out the last one. It used to be that if a business lasted longer than five years it had a pretty good chance of succeeding. Now if a business has been around for that long without a major reinvention of itself or new market direction it's at high risk of failure or going in to a death spiral.

Capitalizing on Chaos

With that in mind, you need to be looking forward. Businesses will be changing directions often, reinventing themselves, coming and going, and you need to fit into all that chaos and be of great value. All these gyrations really lead to the opportunities of the future. If businesses are coming and going on a three, four, or five year cycle then there will be a lot of value for someone who understands instant market penetration and extremely fast business growth. Just as important will be those that know how to wind down a business in the quickest and most profitable way. These are just two examples, food for thought of what opportunities may come and what the new career market may look like.

In many regards, I believe this is a time when we get to have some say in how things play out, but our suggestions must be adaptable to the ever-changing shape of the future. I think the days of traditional education and training are going by the wayside because by the time something is known well enough to be taught it could very well be obsolete. This is not meant to be taken as a blanket statement, as some sectors will remain long-term like gas, oil, healthcare, food, etc., and thus benefit from traditional educational paths. But within even these stable industries, there will be new shifts that will create opportunities. Those that find them and take action will prosper. The other option (for those that don't get up to speed and adapt) is the likely possibility of being commoditized and falling closer to or fully into poverty.

Business

This is the most commonly used method to build wealth quickly. That being said, it's not something that fits everyone's personality, lifestyle, and skills. Therefore, in my mind it's not the be-all and end-all solution to growing wealth. Many would disagree with this, and if you pay attention at all you will see many ads and offers about how to make a bunch of money running your own business.

I love business and have been in it most of my adult life. I also believe it will hold the most opportunities for building substantial wealth in the foreseeable future. But that doesn't mean it will be easily available to the average person or right for everyone.

This is not a business development course, but I want to share with you a few of my thoughts on the subject for those of you who are considering or will be using the business option for building your career income.

Right now in the US the laws and regulations in place are so burdensome that it's almost impossible to be a small business and comply with them all. I'm not talking about the laws that prevent businesses from robbery and fraud. Those regulations are healthy and have their place. Typically, when deregulation comes up one party will be talking about those laws while the deregulating party will be talking about the laws that just create massive and unnecessary obstacles for small business owners.

This all plays into the hands of the big businesses, the ones that are making extreme profits with little to no competition from the little guys. The way this works in favor of the big companies is that they have deep pockets and can afford to hire experts to handle all the legalities while they focus on making money. A small business, on the other hand, rarely has the financial resources to hire this work out. This leaves the owners or other key personnel spending their time trying to figure it out rather than focusing on the parts of their business that make money.

This extra challenge leads to many failures of small businesses and even more that never get started. This reduces competition for the big guys, which leads to a few ultra-wealthy large corporations and many would-be business owners having to take lower paying jobs at these larger companies. In the end, through misinformation or a lack of a clear understanding this causes many voters who want to support small businesses to actually allow laws to be written that are putting them out of business.

While the intent of keeping businesses from robbery and fraud is noble, most new laws put on the books these days do not protect the consumer. They are used to grow the government, raise taxes, and protect big businesses. Large corporations even use lobbyists to manipulate the laws into those that make it harder for small businesses to compete. This is not a conspiracy theory—these facts are easily proven.

Having said that, in the near future many may have to enter the business world and become experts at figuring all this out just to find a decent financial opportunity. Below are a few things to take into consideration if you are thinking about starting a business. Many people have opinions about owning a business although they may have never run one personally. Some of those thoughts include, "if you own a business, you don't have to work hard," and "you can easily make a lot of money." Those are both commonly accepted ideas but rarely are they true.

Stress

Unless you have ran a business before, you are probably underestimating the amount of stress that can be involved. Keeping up with government regulations, cash flow, taxes, employees, and so on can be an overwhelming task sometimes. The bigger your company gets, the more potential complications and the higher risk you have.

You may get into business with the hopes that you will make money. Once you are in it, your thoughts may shift to hoping the company makes enough money so that you can at least afford to make payroll (so your employees can take care of their families). You making money may become secondary since now not only are you responsible for paying your bills, but your continued success or failure will determine if your employees can pay theirs. There are many paradigm shifts a new business owner will go through, some good and some not so great.

Free Time

Most people see successful business people and think, "Wow, it must be nice. They come and go as they please, taking long vacations to great destinations." Those are perceptions based on looking from the outside in at a successful business. But in reality there are many businesses that are just getting started, don't have enough cash flow, are in a growth mode, or are currently transitioning (which leaves the owner with little to no free time). They may actually be stressed out and working around the clock.

Even those that may appear free because they are not stuck behind their desk usually have their minds filled with thoughts about new products, business strategies, employee conflicts, cash flow, and other things. These thoughts stick with the business owner (regardless of size) 24-7, so even when they are home with their family they are often still "on the clock." This can be a substantial burden. Personally, I have gone through many variations of free time in my life, but my least favorite was losing sleep and not being fully present around my family.

There have been many times when I missed a steady paycheck and the luxury of being able to clock out and go home for the night without work still weighing on my mind. Anyone considering running a business needs to clearly understand and think through the impact it will have on their free time and family life. Owning a business has had great benefits for me and allowed me the flexibility to travel to many countries around the world, but that hasn't always been the case.

What is right for one person may not be right for another, so think things through and make sure that it's something you truly want. Too often, we start counting dollars and dreaming about all the money that could be made ours without regard for all the work, stress, and time that it takes to actually reap the rewards.

Passion

One of the things I am most adamant about when talking to friends or clients that are considering getting into business is making sure it's something they love and have a passion for. I personally had a sad experience. I built a very successful business that I had no passion for. I built it for the money, and I built it because I could. In the end, I had a good moneymaker that I would ultimately come to not care about (and eventually walk away from). I didn't have a passion for what I was doing and my heart wasn't in it. Even with the financial success, I got little fulfillment out of what I was doing.

Many people start a business for the money, but I have learned not to look at the money first. It's essential that you can find a way to make the numbers work and that they meet your goals, but there are many ways to build money into a business. On the other hand, if you don't enjoy what you're doing no amount of money will ever be enough to make it rewarding. Your chance for success goes up exponentially when you do something you love and for which you have a passion.

To have passion, your business needs to meet your needs. When you have passion, obstacles that might otherwise seem insurmountable will be powered through with confidence. When you have passion, you will not easily accept failure, and success will at times even seem effortless.

Confidence

Regardless of whether you have it right now, you need to get and maintain your confidence. In a fast-moving, ever-changing society, there will be numerous opportunities to have self-doubt and feel like a lesser person. Employers are in the same boat: they are looking for people with the confidence to help them deal with what lies ahead. Sometimes job security requires you to be a little assertive and show some leadership skills even if you're not in a leadership position.

Having confidence and the ability to be assertive when needed will help keep you from getting pushed around, stepped on, or falling into the cracks. As I mentioned before, what's "right" is primarily based on someone's perception of things and with things changing fast, "right" is a moving target. Having the confidence and awareness of these changes can give you a winning edge.

There are some good programs out there that can help you develop confidence and interpersonal skills. These are very essential skills for success and are aspects of our lives that are changeable, so work to be the best you can at them. I have no problem with someone that says they can be better and will (or are) taking steps to advance themselves with "self help." Imagine if we all admitted we could be better people and sought out the tools to help ourselves strengthen our weaknesses.

On the other hand, I have issues with those that think they are perfect and have no room for personal growth. To me, that's a sign of ignorance. We (hopefully) spend a minimum of twelve years in school, and what are we doing there? That is twelve years full of self-help where we are developing ourselves into stronger individuals. When you go to get training to become a realtor, what are you doing? You are engaging in a self-help activity to open up more opportunities by developing new skills. That's a commendable action and should be encouraged, not ridiculed.

Buck the Trend

Don't be afraid to "buck the trend" and go against what others say or think. Taking an alternative path often opens up new opportunities and in an economic time when those are limited doing something different may be your saving grace. I'm not saying to do the opposite of something just to be different, but if you can find a way to do something better or add some additional value to a situation, you will be deserving of more.

Too often we gravitate towards what others recommend or what large groups are already doing. When you think about it, it makes a lot of sense because there is already social proof that makes it appear to be less risky. Even if it doesn't work out you can say, "Well, everyone else was doing it," or even "It seemed like a good idea at the time." That may help you feel better about a bad decision, but the consequences are not going to be any less severe.

Taking the road less traveled or cutting in a new path may be met with skepticism and concern from family, friends, and others we may trust and look to for guidance. Listen to their advice, test it against your plan, and then move forward accordingly. But honestly, when you venture into the unknown there will be few that can give you "good advice" because they too lack experience in the area and *that* is exactly where a lot of opportunity lies. The fact that it's unknown will keep a lot of people from discovering it, and most that do will lack the confidence to take the risk on something unproven.

The trend doesn't have to be of major consequence. It could be as simple as trying out a new filing system at work that you feel would save time. You can push for giving it a try and if you are right you will have added value that causes your superiors to recognize you as a thinker who is improving their company. In the worst case, if it's a flop I would venture to say most employers would appreciate your efforts towards making their company better, being willing to step up, and actually suggesting something different.

Sir Richard Branson, the billionaire founder of the Virgin Empire (which includes an international airline and cell phone company, among other things), attributes a lot of the company's continued success to the fact that they have an attitude that supports trying new things. If an employee has a new idea, the environment and attitude is supportive of trying it and if it's a success, great! If not, they are not criticized or faulted, they just learn from it and move on. This keeps the Virgin employees looking for great new ideas, which in turn keeps the company exciting and cutting edge.

Job Change

In the past, a job change was a great chance to accelerate income growth. Although possibly a higher risk proposition these days, I still believe it can be a wonderful opportunity, especially if you have unique or exceptional skills in an area with high demand. As competition increases for ever-scarce dollars, companies are looking to tune up their operations to give them an edge in creating a better mousetrap.

If your choice is to proceed with a job change, it needs to be well thought out and pursued with a strategy to make you look as valuable as possible to your prospective employer. Your best chance of guaranteed income improvement is in your initial negotiations. Presenting a clear image to your potential employer of the value that you could bring to them and illustrating why you would be worth every dollar you are asking for is essential. It's a terrible strategy to go into an interview focused solely on defense and prepared to get shaken down. I don't think it's a bad idea to be prepared for that, but I strongly believe it's more important to go in offensively with an intention of displaying what you want them to see, then proactively steering the focus in that direction. That way, you'll have a far greater chance of shedding a favorable light on what you have to offer, which typically makes things go much better.

It may be an employer's job to look out for the company's best interests, but that doesn't mean there are any strict guidelines about if or how someone is qualified. If you are looking to move up with your job change, think of how you can add value and meet that company's needs. Review the Seven Human Needs mentioned earlier and make a list of the things you need to articulate during the interview that will clearly show how hiring you will meet both your interviewer's and the company's needs. Your goal is not necessarily to openly say, "Here is how I can meet your needs." You just need to lay out what you can or will do for them (that you know will meet their needs) and let them interpret the benefits. The simple fact that you have already practiced this exercise in your head beforehand will make it more likely that you will hit on relevant, high-impact topics. Take the following two things into consideration.

Aim High

Aim high and make your best case. Don't be afraid to push the limits of what you know and use your poker face to raise the bet, but be prepared for your bet to be called. I think we often get trapped by thinking, "Well, I have never done that," which can make us feel like we can't ask for a certain salary or position. Thinking like that can unnecessarily limit your potential career growth. I know many people that have had the skills to reach for a different job, maybe just from seeing someone else doing it and personally knowing they could do it even better. But they still never challenged themselves to step up and ask for the job simply because they had never done it before. Until you try that job yourself, how could you ever gain any experience in doing it?

I have personally played a few rounds and used my poker face to open up new opportunities that appeared off-limits to me. I just went in knowing that once I won that round the game will have only just begun and it would then be up to me to learn what I needed to and work my butt off. This required me to work some extra unpaid hours to make up for my shortcomings during the learning curve, but I can honestly say this strategy has without a doubt lead to my fastest career advancement. Furthermore, not only did I advance but it also put me in a position to see behind the curtain of what was available on the next rung up the ladder.

Companies don't always want you to move up. They need all the roles filled, so often times the proverbial glass ceiling is in play for those who can't break through. It's not that they are necessarily trying to hold you down to be mean but rather that they just need competent workers at all levels. If you are doing a great job in your role, they may chose to bring someone else in to fill the role above you to avoid having to find and retrain your replacement.

I have found that there are unspoken barriers that (once crossed) can cause you to discover a whole new world of opportunity you never even realized existed. This is one of the reasons why you may look at someone above you and say, "Wow, they have it so good. What's their secret?" Their secret is they are just on the other side of the barrier. Chances are you could do their job just as well if you were given the opportunity, but unless you get lucky or are groomed to work in that position, you aren't likely to be given an easy opportunity to attain it.

This is where bluffing a little and keeping the risk and consequences in mind can give you a chance to break through some barriers. Just remember this warning: if you come up short, you may have walked away from a secure job. Only *you* know your level of skill and competence, so you have to analyze the risk versus the potential reward and make the decision.

Losing Security

This leads us to my second point, a warning. You need to consider the potential security you are giving up by moving away from the known. But honestly, I hate to see people get overly risk adverse and stuck living in what they know. Especially in today's job market, since there is potentially more risk in not chancing it.

As companies cut back and downsize to reduce costs and increase their competitiveness, you could find yourself unexpectedly laid off from what appeared to be a secure job. And unfortunately, you lose a lot of negotiating power when you are unemployed and looking for a job, even if it is due to downsizing. When a company downsizes, they tend to cut their weakest employees first, so a potential employer has to be asking, "Why did they let you go?"

Think about this. Two people are interviewing for a job: one just got laid off from a company, and the other is from the same company but survived the cut. Knowing nothing more than that, who do you think looks more attractive to an employer? I'll tell you which one I would want to be: the one still employed. One, because I have good reason to be seeking a new job (since the company obviously appears distressed or shrinking, at best) and two, I can play up my strengths and show why the company didn't let me go. The interviewing company may also see this as a great opportunity to steal a key person from a competitor who is already operating from a weakened position.

163

Now, consider if you made your move *before* you got laid off. You could, for example, be a dedicated and valuable employee that they have not rewarded with fair pay or any advancement opportunity. There are a lot of reasonable justifications that may be your motivation for seeking new work, higher pay, or a higher position.

Remember, this is a warning about the risk involved in this plan. I'm shining light on the opposite side of the coin, so if you have tenure in your career, a good bond with your boss, good friends you are working with, or some other non-monetary reason to stay, then you may have more to consider than just the prospective in increased income. Consider all the potential consequences of making this type of change. What if you don't like your new coworkers or your new boss is a jerk? I can't give you advice on this as it varies for every individual and situation—heck, for all I know your boss is already a jerk and your coworkers make you the butt of their jokes on a daily basis. Just be wise in your considerations and make sure any moves are forward with a high potential for a positive outcome.

Career Change

It would be great if everyone could choose their ideal career at a young age, pursue training, and maximize their potential in the industry of their dreams. Unfortunately, such is rarely the case. All too often we may or may not realize that we've ended up somewhere unexpected due to someone else's plan, never considering our career choices properly until we are already well invested. This puts us into a position where transitioning away from an area where we have built skills and value will feel like a difficult step backwards.

This delay and lack of planning early on tends to lead to further complications. As we start to set down roots and take on responsibilities such as marriage, kids, housing, debt, cars, and so on, any career change (especially one that requires reducing or losing our income for a period of time) will be much more painful. This will increase the amount of effort and resolve it will take to achieve any desired change.

So all this planning ahead sounds great, but how in the heck can we predict where we will want to be twenty years down the road at an early age? One of the best ways is to rule out where you *don't* want to be. First, set an income goal (which will eliminate a lot of dead-end and limiting career paths). Next, make sure your career goal is in line with your personal nature and values.

Nature

This is a critical aspect in finding a fulfilling career. The last thing you want to do is focus solely on a money target only to reach that goal and find your very sociable self, for example, staring at a computer screen in a cubicle for twelve hours a day. Money will not buy you back all those hours of misery and lost enjoyment you could've gotten from a career that allowed for more human interaction. (Although on the other hand, if you are an introvert and really would be fine with whatever type of work you would be doing in said cubicle, that type of job may be a perfect fit.)

If you're a shy person, for example, have caution going for a sales position that requires great rapport skills and an outgoing personality. Honestly, it's probably going to lead to a lot of discomfort for you and likely even poor job performance. Similarly, if you are an artistic person locked into a structured environment that allows little opportunity to express yourself then you're not likely to be a good long-term fit for that particular career. Keep in mind though, there will probably be times on the move up the ladder when you'll have to do your time *temporarily* in environments that are less than a perfect match for your personality—after all, life is not perfect.

Luckily, scenarios and skills that come naturally to us are usually apparent long before we reach the point of needing to make a choice on our career path. Taking this into consideration can at least help us avoid blatantly poor career choices. Putting focus in an area that has the income potential you need and does not oppose your nature will naturally give you a much greater chance for success.

Values

Another critical area that needs to be taken into consideration is your values. You want to make sure your career goals do not conflict with the things you believe to be important. Doing so is not only crucial, but picking a career that's in line with your values can actually create a flow that will naturally help you reach your goals more easily.

Gravity is obvious to us. Although we know it's there, we cannot defy it. We may work to reduce its pull against us, but ultimately it's far easier to just accept the circumstances and work around it. Recognizing that values have a similar pull allows us to use them to our advantage. *When I run into a client dissatisfied with their career, often times it's due to a conflict with their values.* Unfortunately, those individuals are usually in knee deep before they felt the effects or even realized there was a conflict.

For example, take someone that loves to help people get what they want out of life. Picture them in a sales position for a company that has one goal: **make sales to everyone**, regardless of whether they want or need what you're selling. The product may be great, but you'll still feel guilty when you sell it to someone that you believe didn't really need or want it. This type of scenario is far from a good recipe for success and enjoyment in your career. You may suck it up and do what you have to so you can pay your bills, but internally you will feel guilty, unfulfilled, and unhappy.

It may seem obvious. Why would anyone choose a career that conflicts with their values? Wouldn't they realize the problem pretty quickly and change their direction? You would hope so, but sometimes the conflict doesn't appear when you're taking the first steps of a particular route. Then you hit step four and realize that everything from here on out has completely different dynamics that don't fit your values. What do you do then? You have worked so hard to excel and

166

get to where your pay is finally starting to show some potential. This is where many will fight it, compromising their values to hang on to their investment of time and energy. Even if it ultimately lasts, your career is likely going to be full of negative energy and potentially be emotionally damaging. If it lasts for a while but ends up coming to an end at a later date, you may regret all that time you wasted not seeking a more fulfilling career.

Meeting Your Needs

Out of all the people I've met who love their job and enjoy going to work, they've all had one thing in common: their career is meeting most (if not all) of their Seven Human Needs. This led me to consequently conclude that any fulfilling career will help meet most of your needs. This is important, so let it soak in. *Any fulfilling career will help meet most of your needs.* The people I've met that were miserable in their jobs also ended up having something in common with each other: their jobs met very few of their needs.

The problem most people have is the inability to visualize (and consequently prioritize) the value of their needs. If you ask someone if their job meets their financial needs, they can do the math and easily tell you the answer. On the other hand, if you ask someone if their job meets their intellectual and emotional needs they will likely have no clue how to calculate such a thing (if they even understand what you are talking about). I personally hope you will take a leap of faith for the purpose of this program and evaluate how your career choice may or may not meet your needs.

We have talked a lot about how to evaluate a career, but unfortunately the likelihood is you are already entrenched in your previously chosen path. Hopefully when you read about nature, values, and needs your current career scored high on that list. On the other hand, you might be thinking, "Oh man, what have I done?" If that's the case, don't despair. What's done is done: the past is the past. At least now you have increased your awareness. Embrace the potential of what that means.

If you're in those shoes, welcome to the club. I have been there and it was a sucker punch to the gut, without question. I've made the hard transition (a totally different career path, extensive retraining, and a financial curve that looked like the great depression) and for me the rewards are incalculable. I had literally gotten to a point in my life where I was just so dissatisfied with the limited range of things money and my career had to offer. It felt like some form of cancer, and I just wanted to get away from it. I realized that most of the things I thought were my dreams were actually little more than the *illusion* of a great life, imprinted on me by society and my upbringing. They had nothing to do with my true desires or needs. I no longer valued everything I had worked for years to obtain. Hopefully a little faith in what I'm saying will mean you don't have to spend years of your life searching for the answers to why your career is so unfulfilling.

If you have reached the conclusion that your current path is not the one for you and you need to make a change, congratulations! In these situations it's always the sooner the better. You should explore all the career options that will meet your income goals, compliment your nature, not conflict with your values or beliefs, and will substantially meet all your needs. Don't limit yourself to the fields involving only the experience, skills, and knowledge that you already have. Keep your mind open to finding the ultimate fit and then determine how to get there using the strategies and information provided in this book.

With some cost versus time analysis, you may be able to make a more dramatic change than you think possible and still come out ahead. After all, a life not fully lived and filled with compromise will never be a fulfilling life.

Immediate Career Income Growth Plan

You are going to create a plan for growing your career income by listing the actions you will take within the next twelve months. Your plan may not involve any actual increase in income during this period—in fact, it may actually result in a reduction. But these actions will immediately put you on the shortest path to a career that has the potential to substantially match your personality while meeting your financial desires. If you already earn a great income but your career is unfulfilling, your plan will primarily aim for growth in life balance and satisfaction (which is absolutely ok). Remember, true wealth is not a dollar amount. It's a state of being.

Work through the following few pages to evaluate different careers and determine which one is right for you. Make that career the target of your pursuit. Start by entering your ideal annual income you have previously determined or your adjusted compromise goal.

| My Ideal Annual Income (page 135) | $ _____ |

NOTES :

_____

_____

_____

_____

_____

_____

_____

_____

Meeting My Needs

What will it take for you to fulfill each of your human needs through your career? Take a minute to think it through and write a brief description of the environment, people, and activities you need to best achieve this goal.

Sustenance

In order for me to feel I can be assured of my ability to sustain my lifestyle with my career, I would need:

_____

_____

_____

Connection

To feel connected and dedicated to my career and the people I work with, I would need:

_____

_____

_____

Security

To feel totally secure, have no doubts about my ability to maintain income stability, and know that I will be treated with respect in my career, I would need:

_____

_____

_____

Growth

To feel like I am continually advancing and growing in my career, I would need:

_____

_____

_____

Significance

For me to feel significant and like I am a valuable contributor to my career, I would need:

_____

_____

_____

Esteem

To feel I am engaged in a career that gives me pride and supports my feelings of esteem and self-esteem, I would need:

_____

_____

_____

Inner Peace

For me to feel enthusiastic and at peace in my career, aside from fulfilling my other needs I would need:

_____

_____

_____

Natural Match

One of the most common mistakes people make in choosing a career is not considering their personal nature. Take a minute to describe your ideal career situation regarding the following elements (specifically, as they relate to your nature—your *essential* characteristics and qualities).

Social Environment

What would be your ideal social environment (where you feel the most comfortable and could perform the best)?

_____

_____

_____

Pressure

Some people like challenging environments, perform well under pressure that would crack others, and would get bored if not constantly challenged. How much pressure is comfortable for you?

_____

_____

_____

Environment

Are you someone that feels at home in a static office environment? Would you prefer to travel or be outdoors? Would you like to be part of the support staff, or do you prefer to be the key figure? Do you like board meetings, beaches, or both? What are some key environment-related aspects (physical, mental, etc.) you desire in a career?

_____

_____

_____

Ethics

What moral and ethical boundaries do you need to take into consideration? A vegetarian would not fit in working at a slaughter house. If you cannot tell a lie, don't get a job selling used cars. What are the moral and ethical boundaries that are deal makers and breakers for you?

_____

_____

_____

Career Assets

You likely already have some job or business experience under your belt as well as some applicable skills, abilities, and certifications. These things are what I call your current career assets. They may have significant value, so you should try to leverage them the best you can. Hopefully they will even be applicable in your ultimate career, helping you obtain the best possible starting position. Your ultimate career may not require a field change that jeopardizes the value of these assets, but if it does give serious consideration to where and how they still might be used to create value.

Make a list of your current career assets. This could include years of experience performing certain tasks or in a certain field as well as degrees, certifications, innate abilities, personality traits, relationships, associations, and so on. Think broadly about anything that you have that might be of value as an employee or in a business situation (depending on the direction you choose). These may not all be resume items, but they surely need to be leveraged as much as possible. As you make your list you will probably be surprised at how much you actually have to offer.

PART TWO: TWELVE MONTH REBALANCE

My Career Assets

1. _____

2. _____

3. _____

4. _____

5. _____

6. _____

7. _____

8. _____

9. _____

10. _____

Potential Career Paths

With all those things in mind brainstorm, research, solicit ideas from your acquaintances, and do wherever you can to come up with a list of potential careers that best fit the following four elements.

1) Meets your income goals

2) Fulfills all (or at least most) of your Seven Human Needs

3) Does not drastically conflict with your values, beliefs and/or nature

4) Makes the best use of your current career assets

Maybe you know exactly what you want to do. The list doesn't need to be fully populated. On the other hand, if you are not totally set then take some time and explore all your options. Remember, you will be spending a lot of your time and energy in your career so choose wisely.

Career Options

1. _____
2. _____
3. _____
4. _____
5. _____
6. _____
7. _____
8. _____
9. _____
10. _____

NOTES :

_____
_____
_____
_____
_____
_____
_____
_____
_____
_____
_____

Decide

Now that you have done your research and taken a full inventory of the related information, you need to make a decision. This is a major choice, and you need to think it through carefully. If you want to continue the program further while this information simmers a little bit, skip to the housing section now and come back later.

If you are clear on your verdict, put your decision in ink and follow the next few exercises. Admittedly, your career choice may just be to stay where you are and take actions to excel up the ladder. If that's the case just fill in your current career and then the ideal position and pay as your goals.

My Career Goals

Industry: _____

Position: _____

Income: $ _____

Congratulations!

Whether you chose to just move up or change fields all together to something that better suits your needs and personality, I want to congratulate you on making the first big step. I mean it whole-heartedly. I have been in the same position as you and it took a big change and a lot of commitment to get out of it. Was it worth it? Absolutely, without question! This career change plan is also a great remedy for slowing hair loss and stabilizing your hair color—I can vouch for that. Best wishes moving forward!

"Money does not create a great life, it will only compliment one."

- Daniel Hartjoy

CAREER ACTION PLAN

Now that you have made a decision, you need to make an action plan to quickly and successfully proceed to the next level. Make a list of all the key requirements you need to meet to make this change successful. It may include getting a student loan or cutting costs as your income goes down while you are retraining. Don't worry about the "how" yet, just the "what." If you need more space just write them on a separate sheet of paper. Also, don't worry about how long your list gets. I'm going to show you a powerful method for getting results, so many of the things on your list may happen by default.

Key Requirements for Transition

1. _____
2. _____
3. _____
4. _____
5. _____
6. _____
7. _____
8. _____
9. _____
10. _____
11. _____
12. _____
13. _____
14. _____
15. _____

PART TWO: TWELVE MONTH REBALANCE

Before you go any further write down your feelings about the change you are making. Here are a couple of prompts to guide your writing. And remember, there is a point to every exercise you are given.

What enjoyment and benefits will you receive from making this change? What will your life look like five years from now?

_____

_____

_____

_____

_____

_____

What negative effects and pains will come from *not* making this change? If you don't make this change, what will your life look like five years from now?

_____

_____

_____

_____

_____

_____

Use the following Action Tree method to prioritize and track the key requirements you need to make this change happen. This is a fast and powerful method for making change. Feel free to make as many copies as you need of this form. You may also want to use it to break some key actions down into smaller steps. You can download additional electronic copies at www.WealthBuilderLifestyle.com/tools.

Action Tree

The Action Tree is about taking effective action and creating exceptional results with minimal effort. It's a ten-step method based on the 80/20 rule (also called Pareto's Principle) which essentially states that 20% of the effort you make will create 80% of the results. Therefore you can get a four-to-one return by focusing on the 20% that has the potential to make the largest impact first.

You should have already made a decision about something you want to do or obtain prior to implementing the action tree. A tree is a great metaphor for creating something amazing from virtually nothing. If the right actions are taken with a particular seed (idea), something almost inconceivable can grow. On the other hand, leave that seed untouched in the wrong environment and it will remain nothing more than a seed.

For each of these steps write down the most powerful actions you can take that will generate the most results. There may only be a few for each step but think it through and try to come up with ten for each. Then go through your list and take the most powerful of those to use in the Action Tree.

NOTES :

_____

_____

_____

_____

_____

_____

_____

PART TWO: TWELVE MONTH REBALANCE
Step 1: Plant the Seed

This is the most powerful step because it will take your decision and set it in motion. Make your decision a true commitment by taking action—for example, register your domain name, get a loan, update your resume and send it out to five places, sign a contract, or get some advanced training. This should be something that will create tangible results and firmly commit you to following through. This action should not be easy to change or undo.

1. _____
2. _____
3. _____
4. _____
9. _____

5. _____
6. _____
7. _____
8. _____
10. _____

Step 2: Set the Roots

This should include two power actions that will reinforce your commitment and make sure that you are going to follow through in achieving your goal. They may include getting others involved, giving notice at your job, leasing a building, or something else that makes it harder for you to break your commitment to your goal. **WARNING:** I'm not advising you to do foolish or crazy things (like quit your job) without preparation! Your actions need to make sense and be well thought out.

1. _____
2. _____
3. _____
4. _____
9. _____

5. _____
6. _____
7. _____
8. _____
10. _____

CAREER ACTION PLAN
Step 3: Accelerate Growth

Per the tree metaphor, this step involves fertilizing the soil. This includes taking two more power actions that create a "big splash" in results, essentially hitting turbo mode on your plan to create momentum. These results should greatly accelerate your forward progress towards your goal. Things don't have to be perfect yet.

1. _____   5. _____

2. _____   6. _____

3. _____   7. _____

4. _____   8. _____

9. _____   10. _____

Step 4: Shape Your Results

You've taken massive action and created major results with big hits, and now you need to take some powerful steps towards filling in the voids. What do you need to do to support your big changes? Maybe you need to do a little damage control to get things inline. Maybe you have dedicated all your time and energy into accelerating your education and now it's time to get your outer image in shape. Maybe some new clothes and a makeover are in order to align your newfound inner strength with your outer appearance. Whatever it may be, this should help balance your massive growth initiated in Step Three.

1. _____   5. _____

2. _____   6. _____

3. _____   7. _____

4. _____   8. _____

9. _____   10. _____

Step 5: Perfect Your Outcome

These final actions are going to help clean up the mess and polish off your achievement. When you trim a tree you make it look great, but it makes a big mess. It may be perfect, but other areas may need to be put back in shape for you to feel the full value of the change. What power actions can you take to polish off the little details so your new goal can become a lasting part of your new life?

1. _____   5. _____

2. _____   6. _____

3. _____   7. _____

4. _____   8. _____

9. _____   10. _____

Conclusion

Remember, I said the most powerful 20% of your efforts can create 80% of your results. In business I have watched many business owners get caught up with trying to perfect little details that have very little (if any) overall impact on their business. Keep the broad picture in mind, always focusing on the most powerful 20% that will get you the most results in achieving your goals. Half of what we tend to think we need to do doesn't really need to be done.

NOTES :

_____

_____

_____

_____

_____

CAREER ACTION PLAN

Use the following form to plan, track, and monitor progress on your goal.

	Career Goal Action Tree		
	Goal _____		
STEP	**Progress Tracker** shade one box for every action completed	☐ ☐ ☐ ☐ ☐ ☐ ☐ ☐ ☐ ☐	
	Plant the Seed – Write one action that will turn an idea into a real decision.		
1	Your Seed Action	_____	☐
	Set the Roots – Take two power actions that will further commit you to your goal.		
2	First Influential, Root-Setting Action	1. _____	☐
	Second Influential, Root-Setting Action	2. _____	☐
	Accelerate Growth – Take two more power actions that will produce massive growth.		
3	First Influential Fertilization Action	1. _____	☐
	Second Influential Fertilization Action	2. _____	☐
	Shape Your Results – Take two more power actions to fill voids and refine your approach.		
4	First Influential Shaping Action	1. _____	☐
	Second Influential Shaping Action	2. _____	☐
	Perfect Your Outcome – Take two more power actions that clean up any remaining mess.		
5	First Influential Clean-Up Action	1. _____	☐
	Second Influential Clean-Up Action	2. _____	☐

Check the appropriate box after each action is completed.

HOUSING

Typically one of our biggest expenses (if not the biggest) is our home, whether rented or purchased. I saved this part for after the other easy adjustments to your spending because it will likely take months or even the entire year to bring this in line.

This is often a painful area to fix. There are two primary ways I advise people to approach this depending on if you are renting or buying. Sometimes it may even make sense to do a blended approach if one direction is not blatantly the best.

Start by entering the current amount you spend and the guideline amount you are trying to get your housing cost in line with below. If your current housing expenses are within the guideline amount, congratulations! Feel free to skip the rest of this section, although you may still want to read through it just to understand the concept in case you may be able to apply this philosophy in other areas or at another time.

Current Housing Expenses (pg 96)	$ _____
Guideline Housing Expenses (pg 96)	$ _____
Housing Cost Reduction Necessary (current expenses – guideline expenses)	$ _____

NOTES :

_____

_____

_____

_____

_____

Renting

If you are currently a renter there are two initial options for getting your numbers inline. First, you could evaluate a potential move to a less expensive rental arrangement. This would be the easiest method mathematically, but may not be possible based on the region you live in. Second, you could buy a home that fits within your budget.

As you get into the wealth building part of the program you will see that this is not necessarily a permanent life commitment. Over the long term, I believe renting is a sucker's bet. It may be cheaper today compared to buying a home, but you will always be at the mercy of the rental market. Costs in the rental market will continue to go up and can even skyrocket with an economic boom—just ask anyone from Silicon Valley in California. This may not be a problem for you if you are earning and a part of that boom, but if you are retired and on a fixed income, a boom could lead to your doom and unnecessarily put you in a bad situation.

Option One: Relocate

Our goal is to get your costs down without dramatically impacting your quality of life. I'm not advising you to do something like move into an unsafe area with poor schools to save a buck (as the real consequences of doing something like are not worth it). On the other hand, doing an honest evaluation may open up some better options. Maybe you could consider a different location, a smaller unit, or a building with fewer luxurious amenities. Do some market research and enter the rental cost for any potential rental option that would be less than what you are currently paying.

Current Rental Cost	$
New Rental Cost	$
Monthly Amount Saved by Moving (current rent – new rent)	$

We are not going to factor in the moving costs because the goal is to get you in balance within twelve months and that would be a one-time expense. It may be a minor setback, but if you get in balance the cost will be offset by your wealth building progress in the near future.

Pros of Option One

Enter the five advantages you would benefit from by making this move. When considering your new location take into account the schools, your location of work, and other places you will frequent like stores, parks, and recreational options. Considering these factors can help reduce your costs in other areas and make the change more appealing. Would it positively affect any of your relationships with friends or family? When you consider your relationship consequences, consider the possibility of maybe breaking or weakening some ties with people in your life that aren't really contributing in a positive way. You may also be able to move closer to some that are positive influences on you.

1. _____
2. _____
3. _____
4. _____
5. _____

Cons of Option One

Enter the five likely disadvantages that would come from making this move. Remember to consider all of the things we did for the benefits list above. How would this adversely impact your quality of life?

1. _____
2. _____
3. _____
4. _____
5. _____

Is the relocating option a viable way to get you in balance or at least substantially closer without destroying your quality of life? Remember, this is a short-term fix on the way to a richer and more fulfilling life. A little sacrifice in the short term can greatly accelerate your advancement towards a better future.

Option Two: Buy a Home

Look at purchasing a home rather than renting. As I write this, home loan interest rates are extremely low and housing costs are down due to the economic slowdown. This may very well be one of the best times to enter the housing market for years to come. Sure, the economy may be slow for some time but rental costs are not likely to decline much (if any), so buying a place at or near the same cost as renting could be your best bet.

I tend to advise most people to try to get through the rebalancing phase before buying as the reduction in short-term debt and better financial balance will make their credit look better. That being said, if you have the means and it makes sense to do it now then go for it.

We will be talking more about home buying and building wealth with real estate later in this course so be sure to finish it before actually making a real estate purchase. To ensure you can make the best possible decision, do some research in your local real estate market to see what your options are for getting into a home versus renting. Are there some houses out there that will suite your needs and work within your budget? Feel free to contact a realtor and let them know about your situation. You may be surprised at what they can come up with for you and they will be more than happy to do this at no cost.

If there is a suitable home out there that falls within your budget you are likely going to be referred to a mortgage broker. They can help you evaluate whether or not you currently qualify for a loan and what the actual costs would be. Don't feel obligated to actually use the recommended broker if you do go this direction. Once you know the anticipated purchase price, you can compare numerous mortgage options (both local and online) to seek the best deal possible. A quick word of caution: don't let a bunch of them run credit checks as too many inquiries within a short period of time can negatively affect your credit score.

One other thing to consider if you're moving from renting to buying is that as you become a wealth builder your finances will be improving. So tying up your credit and energy in the home you can afford now may limit your options to get into a more desirable home later.

Do a little research and fill in the boxes below to see if you could meet your housing cost reduction by purchasing a home. If it will cost you more than what you are currently paying, enter the Monthly Cost Difference as a negative (so you at least know the difference).

Current Housing Cost	$
New Home Cost	$
Monthly Cost Difference (current housing – new home cost)	$

This may not be a feasible option at the moment but even if the cost of purchasing will be more expensive than renting do this exercise and finish your research. One advantage of buying is you will be earning equity each month and that counts as investment contribution (which may make the numbers work out). With any luck, your new home will also be appreciating and giving you additional free wealth.

NOTES :

_____

_____

_____

PART TWO: TWELVE MONTH REBALANCE
Pros of Option Two

Enter the five advantages you would benefit from by making this move. When considering your new location take into account the schools, your location of work, and other places you need to travel to like stores, parks, and recreational options. Taking these factors into account can help reduce your costs in other areas and make the change more appealing. Also, would it positively affect any of your relationships with friends or family? When you consider your relationship consequences, consider the possibility of maybe breaking or weakening some ties with people in your life that aren't really contributing in a positive way. You may also be able to move closer to some that are beneficial to you.

1. _____
2. _____
3. _____
4. _____
5. _____

Cons of Option Two

Enter the five likely disadvantages that would come from making this move. Remember to consider all of the things you did for the benefits list above. How would this adversely impact your quality of life?

1. _____
2. _____
3. _____
4. _____
5. _____

Is Option Two a viable way to get you substantially closer to being in balance without totally destroying your quality of life?

Home Buying

If you are currently purchasing a home, you may often be referred to as a homeowner. Although we have adopted this term and consider home ownership a fact, it's very misleading. The reality for many is that if they calculated the length of the loan left and then multiplied it by their payment amount they would likely still have to pay *more* than the home is currently worth before they ever really owned it. We are going to look into a number of home buying options that will allow you to get closer to (if not fully in) balance with your guideline. One of the great things about owning (or at least being in control of) a home is that you can use your house any way you like, potentially even in a way that can create additional income. We'll be examining four different options.

Option One: Refinance

Is there a refinancing option that can help get your numbers inline with your goals? Research your options online and talk to a mortgage broker to find out how much you could reduce your monthly costs via refinancing and what the total transaction cost would be.

Do not make the mistake of doing a singular evaluation—just a lower payment—which your lender will likely have you focus on. For instance, extending your loan may reduce your payment even after adding in the refinance transaction cost, but may increase the overall cost you will pay for your home—thus making it a bad financial decision. That would be a plan for people with a poor financial education.

Use the following simple worksheet to evaluate your refinancing options. Determine if there is one that will provide you with a solution that makes your home more affordable today without increasing your overall cost. Fill in the boxes and complete the formulas to see how different options really compare. Not only will this help you compare assorted loan options, but it will also give you

PART TWO: TWELVE MONTH REBALANCE

an idea of how much you're really going to end up paying for your home (which is much different than the purchase price most people focus on). You will need to go online and use an amortization calculator or talk to a mortgage broker to complete this step.

Option One Analysis				
Item or Calculation	Current Mortgage	Option One	Option Two	Option Three
Loan Balance	$_____	$_____	$_____	$_____
Fees Added to Loan	N/A	$_____	$_____	$_____
Total Loan Amount	$_____	$_____	$_____	$_____
New Payment	N/A	$_____	$_____	$_____
Determine the monthly cost to pay off your refinancing fees in twelve months.				
One-time Fees	N/A	$_____	$_____	$_____
One-time Fees ÷ 12	N/A	$_____	$_____	$_____
		+	+	+
New Payment	N/A	$_____	$_____	$_____
Ongoing Payment (new or existing)	$_____	$_____	$_____	$_____
Enter new and existing interest rates to see the real cost versus interest rate difference.				
Interest Rate (APR)	_____%	_____%	_____%	_____%

NOTES :

_____

_____

_____

_____

_____

On the next table, multiply the total number of loan payments required to pay off the loan times the payment amount. This will determine the total of all your payments which will give you a better idea of what each option will cost long term. Remember to use only the months left when calculating your existing loan amount.

Option One Analysis (cont.)				
Loan Length	_____	_____	_____	_____
	× 12 =	× 12 =	× 12 =	× 12 =
Months to Pay Off Loan	_____	_____	_____	_____
	×	×	×	×
Ongoing Payment (from previous form)	$_____	$_____	$_____	$_____
	=	=	=	=
Total of All Payments	$_____	$_____	$_____	$_____
This is the **real total cost** of your refinance options. Add the total of all your payments to any one-time fees that will not be rolled in to your new loan.				
Total of All Payments + One-Time Fees	$_____	$_____	$_____	$_____

The most important numbers you will want to look at in the last two worksheets are in the shaded boxes, and the darkest box is ultimately the most important. You should still look over the other boxes to get a feel for how different interest rates and loan lengths can affect your payments and the total amount you will need to pay. You will want to make sure that if you do have to pay some loan fees you will be able to cover the additional amount to get them paid off during the Twelve-Month Rebalance. Otherwise, the new payment amount may be deceptive and not actually the best way to help you get in balance. If you roll the payments into your loan you will want to look at the overall impact on the total you will pay for your home.

Although I advise people to pay off their loans in fifteen years or less, I typically recommend they get a thirty-year mortgage. With that in mind, if you have for example seventeen years left on your existing mortgage I would never advise you to take out a new thirty-year loan to make it more affordable. It may still make sense to refinance to a twenty-year loan if the interest rate is lower and the total loan costs are equal to or less than your current loan. Unfortunately, banks will not typically be interested in loans of a random length and a fifteen-year loan may not do enough to make your payments work out (even with a lower interest rate).

Option Two: Sell Your Existing Home

I know this may be a sad option to even consider, but if you're not currently building wealth at a rate that's in line with the Wealth Builder Lifestyle, it could very well be necessary. If you're substantially outside of the guidelines because your mortgage is eating you alive, you may need to consider selling your home and downsizing.

These days people tend to have nicer houses than they can afford which leads to the waste of their potential wealth building cash on home loan interest. Sure, you can write it off, but that is another misnomer (just like the misconceptions about being a homeowner). A write-off is just that: you are writing off money you no longer have. I would much rather pay 25% in income taxes and keep $75 than write off $100 to avoid paying the $25 in taxes.

Selling and downsizing can lead to having a home paid off much quicker. Then you can upgrade to a more expensive home later as your wealth increases and you can afford to do it while maintaining positive wealth creation.

In the following worksheet you will see a few examples based on different hypothetical scenarios regarding downsizing. These three scenarios, although hypothetical, are 100% possible and only require varying actions. They assume a starting home value of $300,000 with $71,600 in equity, meaning the payoff balance of the loan is $228,400. The amazing thing about the two wealth builder options is they both assume an initial equity loss of $31,500. Even with that initial loss, by the end of the 18-year period covered your wealth would be over

$55,000 higher and it wouldn't cost you one penny more. The increase is made simply by living the Wealth Builder Lifestyle.

Sadly, most people stay locked into the "no change" scenario due to a lack of financial education, laziness, or an unwillingness to live a little more humbly. The result of that thinking is that over 18 years they will spend $328,320 to gain $228,400 in wealth, not even breaking even with the value of their investment contribution.

In all fairness, I have included no real estate appreciation (which you could expect to add to your total investment value). I left out appreciation for simplicity and because it can vary greatly. That being said, you would receive more appreciation on a higher cost home. This also works the opposite way, as some people are now very familiar with. Over the last five years many homes in the United States have lost 25% to 50% in value and the higher the cost the larger the loss. I prefer to look at your home as a security investment that you don't expect to make a huge return on but rather hope to see consistent positive growth in value while striving for complete ownership as quickly as possible.

Option Two Example			
(Example based on 4.5% APR)			
Existing Home		**New Home**	
Likely Sale Amount (market value)	$300,000	Purchase Price	$210,000
Sale Cost (realtor and closing costs)	$24,000	Buyer's Fees (closing cost)	$7,500
Existing Loan Payoff	$228,400	Down Payment (proceeds from home sale)	$47,600
Net Proceeds From Sale (sale amount – sale cost – loan payoff)	$47,600	**New Loan Amount**	$169,900
Equity (sale amount – loan balance)	$71,600	**Equity** (purchase price – loan balance)	$40,100
Monthly Mortgage Payment	$1,520 ×	Monthly Mortgage Payment	$1,149 ×
Remaining Loan Length (in months)	216 =	Loan Length (in months)	216 =
Total of Remaining Payments	**$328,320**	**Total of Remaining Payments**	**$248,184**

195

PART TWO: TWELVE MONTH REBALANCE

In the previous example you initially lose $31,500 in equity which appears to be a step backwards. But looking down the road to the time when your existing home is paid off you will see that you will have spent $328,320 dollars to have a $300,000 asset (no inflation accounted for). On your new home, you will have paid $248,184 to own your $210,000 asset. In this way, it still would appear more sensible to keep your existing home and just suck up the larger payments. That is, until you apply the following Wealth Builder Lifestyle strategies.

We are going to compare two alternatives to the option of doing nothing. For the first, we will invest the difference between the two loan options into something with an anticipated 10% return for the full loan length of 216 months. For the second, we will follow an accelerated payoff plan (paying the current monthly mortgage payment of $1,520 instead of the new $1,149 payment to pay the loan off quicker) and then invest for the last 71 months. The total amount paid over the 18-year period (216 months) is the same for all three of these options. The only thing that changes is the method of spending which is made possible by downsizing into a more affordable home that will allow a small contribution to a Wealth Builder Lifestyle. The total investment in each scenario is 216 × $1,520 for a grand total of $328,320.

NOTES :

_____

_____

_____

_____

_____

_____

196

HOUSING

Option Two Example (cont.)			
(Investments based on 10% return)			
Investing the Difference		**Accelerated Payoff Then Invest**	
Total Monthly Investment	$371	Monthly Mortgage Payment	$1,520
Contribution Length (in months)	216	Loan Length (months)	145
Total Pre-Interest Investment	$80,136	**Total of Remaining Payments**	$220,400
Total Investment Value at 10%	**$213,844**	**Accelerated Payoff Savings**	$27,784
		Monthly Investment	$1,520
		Investment Length (in months)	71
		Total Pre-Interest Investment	$107,920
		Total Investment Value at 10%	$145,552
Wealth Impact After 18 Years			
Current Home (no change)			**$300,000**
New Home (Investing the Difference)			**$423,844**
New Home (Accelerated Payoff Plus Investment)			**$355,552**

Option Two Analysis

Use the following form to enter your actual information and evaluate the downsizing concept. One other thing to consider when doing this evaluation is that I used the purchase price as the new home value in the examples. There are currently many foreclosures and distressed properties on the market, so if you did your due diligence you could likely purchase your new home well below its current market value. This could give you the potential to improve your equity position rather than take a loss like the example shows.

NOTES :

_____

_____

_____

_____

PART TWO: TWELVE MONTH REBALANCE

Option Two Analysis	
Existing Home	**New Home**
Likely Sale Amount (market value) $_____	Purchase Price $_____
Sale Cost (realtor and closing costs) $_____	Buyer's Fees (closing cost) $_____
Existing Loan Payoff $_____	Down Payment (proceeds from home sale) $_____
Net Proceeds From Sale (sale – sale cost – loan payoff) $_____	**New Loan Amount** $_____
Equity (sale amount – loan balance) $_____	**Equity** (purchase price – loan balance) $_____
Monthly Mortgage Payment $_____	**Monthly Mortgage Payment** $_____
×	×
Remaining Loan Length (in months) $_____	**Loan Length** (in months) $_____
=	=
Total of Remaining Payments $_____	**Total of Remaining Payments** $_____

Use online interest and amortization calculators for the following form.

Investing the Difference	Accelerated Payoff Then Invest
Total Monthly Investment $_____	Monthly Mortgage Payment $_____
Contribution Length (months) $_____	Loan Length (months) $_____
Total Pre-Interest Investmen $_____	Total of Remaining Payments $_____
Total Investment Value $_____	**Accelerated Payoff Savings** $_____
	Monthly Investment $_____
	Investment Length (in months) $_____
	Total Pre-Interest Investment $_____
	Total Investment Value $_____

Wealth Impact After _____ Years

Current Home (no change)	$_____
New Home (Investing the Difference)	$_____
New Home (Accelerated Payoff Plus Investment)	$_____

Option Three: Buy an Additional Home

Buy another, less expensive home. If you have a larger home than you can currently afford but don't want to or can't sell it, consider this option. Rent your existing home out and either buy another more affordable one or just rent a cheaper home temporarily. Sounds crazy, right? If you have a great, beautiful home why would you want to move out and rent something else? If you can't afford it but the numbers work, you can still keep your dream home. Maybe in three to five years your income will increase enough to make that home payment suitable for a Wealth Builder Lifestyle. The benefit of renting another place for yourself is that you are not locked into another loan and can move out at the end of your lease. The long-term drawback, of course, is that the rent is likely to continue going up.

On the other hand, if you choose to buy another home you are locked into a payment at today's price and over the next few years as your income increases the payments will get easier to make. You will still maintain your interest write-offs and even gain some others. I know I said you don't want to write-off money, but honestly my point was to not write-off money just for the sake of it. Talk to your accountant (or find one) to get all the details regarding the advantages and disadvantages of doing so in your local area. If you don't have an accountant, you should find one that you can start building a relationship with because as you get wealthier you will certainly have a need for one. A good accountant will easily offset their cost and then some in savings, which makes them better than free.

Write-offs are great when they make sense. You can't get a write-off for the money you spend for rent, so if your house payment is similar then being able to write-off part of it makes a lot of sense.

Another benefit of buying an additional house is that you will be building equity in two homes while only paying for one. The principle paid down on both houses and any appreciation will continue to add to your wealth. So not only will you reduce your housing costs, but you will actually have renters buying a home for you as well. Essentially you'll be using the bank's money to build wealth.

I have friends that have chosen to rent out their dream home and live in one of their rental houses. In one particular situation, they were able to rent their home out for $1,000 more per month than their expenses. In addition to that, they moved into a rental house which cost them less than $1,000 per month. With just that change they were able to go from paying $2,500 a month for housing to living for free and actually getting paid a few hundred dollars. It was a little bit of a lifestyle change, but they used it to their advantage to free up money and as a result were able to spend a year sailing their boat in the Mediterranean.

Depending on home values and rental rates in your area, this may or may not be a good option for you. Your credit and current interest rates will also affect the feasibility of this method of wealth creation. The results from living a more humble standard of living in the short term can lead to a much richer future in the long term.

Option Three Analysis

The following two forms are valuable tools that you can use to evaluate purchasing another less expensive home to live in while renting out your current home.

Do a little market research for your area and input the answers. You don't have to go to extreme lengths initially, just try to get your estimates close. If this approach looks like it will work out and make sense for you, then you can tighten up the numbers. You will also need an amortization calculator which can be found online to determine your approximate new mortgage payment.

Option Three Analysis	
Existing Home	**Potential Second Home**
Potential Monthly Rent $ _____	Existing Mortgage Payment $ _____
Monthly Rent × 11 = $ _____	**New Mortgage Payment** $ _____ -
÷	
(allows 8% for vacancy) 12	=
=	
Monthly Rental Income $ _____	**Monthly Amount Saved** $ _____
Monthly Mortgage Payment $ _____	One-Time Cost
Other Expenses (not Covered by Renters) $ _____	(down payment and other) $ _____
Combine all expenses	Equity (house value – new loan amount) $ _____ -
	=
Combined Monthly Expenses $ _____	**Amount Lost by Purchase** (will likely be negative) $ _____
Subtract Monthly Expenses from Rent Income	**Recovery Cost** ÷ 12 = $ _____
Approximate Monthly Net (gain or loss) $ _____	**New Mortgage Payment + Recovery Cost** $ _____

It is likely that you will have some uncovered purchase costs that are not offset by equity. Ideally, we would like to get these paid off with savings within the first year. Unfortunately, it may not be possible to completely pay off all these costs within the first twelve months. For simplicity in this analysis we will figure out the uncovered balance and compare it against any future gains.

There are numerous ways to evaluate the cost of dealing with the remaining balance. You will have to do the math and evaluate how quickly to pay down any carryover balance. It may make sense to just continue paying steadily after the first year until it's fully paid off by deferring investing or reducing the original amount being paid and investing the difference.

A word of caution: if you defer paying off the carryover, give careful consideration to the lack of financial flexibility this will cause. Extending the length of time you will be carrying additional debt payments will limit your ability to easily reduce your overhead should you fall into hard financial times. You can easily suspend your investment contributions during a hard time, so knocking out your remaining purchase expenses before investing may have some merit.

With the addition of your new home you will be gaining equity in two properties while reducing monthly expenses which will allow you to build some investment wealth. Use the following form to calculate your potential wealth creation.

Option Three Potential Wealth Creation		
Existing Mortgage Payment $_____	Existing Mortgage Payment $_____	
−	−	
New Mortgage Payment + Recovery Cost (previous page) $_____	New Mortgage Payment $_____	
=	=	
Monthly Net $_____	**Mortgage Monthly Net** $_____	
× 12	+ Approximate Monthly Net (from previous chart) $_____	
=	=	
Total Uncovered Expenses (after 1st year) $_____	**Total Available to Invest** (after 1st year) $_____	

On the following form, use an online amortization calculator and your loan terms to determine your Real Estate Equity wealth creation potential over time (top half). For each corresponding time period, add the investment wealth created during that same time period (lower left) to the real estate equity gains (top half) and enter the totals in the lower right.

HOUSING

Use an online compound interest calculator to determine your investment wealth creation possibility over time. Use the Total Available to Invest as your monthly contribution amount. Subtract the Total Uncovered Expenses from your calculations to determine the true wealth created. In addition, exclude twelve months from all investment calculations as that money has already been used to offset the money lost during the purchase.

Option Three Wealth Increase			
Real Estate Equity Gains			
Term	Existing	New	Combined
5 Years (60 months)	$_____	$_____	$_____
10 Years (120 months)	$_____	$_____	$_____
20 Years (240 months)	$_____	$_____	$_____
30 Years (360 months)	$_____	$_____	$_____

Investment Wealth Gains	Value	Time	Existing	New + Inv.	Combined
5 Year (based on only 4 years)	$_____	5 Years	$_____	$_____	$_____
10 Year (based on only 9 years)	$_____	10 Years	$_____	$_____	$_____
20 Year (based on only 19 years)	$_____	20 Years	$_____	$_____	$_____
30 Year (based on only 29 years)	$_____	30 Years	$_____	$_____	$_____

Enter the amounts from your New [Asset Equity] + Inv. [Investment] inputs above into the chart below in order to create a summary of your potential wealth creation over time.

Wealth Increase Summary for New Strategy			
5 Years $_____	10 Years $_____	20 Years $_____	30 Years $_____

It's always important to give serious consideration before taking on any additional debt. Although this can be a great method of leveraging other people's money (OPM) and building wealth, it can also create added financial risk.

Some things you should consider are how secure your job is, if you have an adequate amount of money set aside in the event of a setback, and if the long-term benefits make the risk worth it. The majority of people will successfully build wealth when using this method, but it should not be jumped into carelessly.

Option Four: Employing Your Home

Use your home to generate money. If you're willing to be open-minded and consider all your options, you may have income opportunities available to you that you are not currently capitalizing on.

Renting out a spare bedroom may bring in the few hundred dollars needed to get you inline. Remember, the most powerful principles in this program are not based on making big, one-time hits but rather consistent little ones that add up to be substantial over time. You may not want to give up your privacy for a few hundred dollars a month, and I get that, but this may be one of the easiest ways to initially get in balance and start building wealth.

There are a lot of students and single individuals out there that just need an affordable place to call home. I know many people that have rented to foreign exchange students, elderly folks, and other good people that just need a chance. I'm not saying that it will always work out great, only that from what I have seen it has been a positive life experience for those that have done it. When you add in the little financial boost it creates, this can be a great option.

If you have land or perhaps a detached garage you don't necessarily use, you may opt to rent it out for someone to store a boat or RV. If you have the space, you may even want to rent out a place for someone to live in their RV on your property. These things may sound a little crazy, but if you're willing to get creative there are numerous opportunities to make a little extra money. You just need to think outside the box.

I can't say what is right for you or your situation. However, if you haven't thought through how you could have your assets building wealth for you, I would highly recommend looking into it. In the last 20 years or so opportunity and money have come pretty easily. As we move into the future and things tighten up, we need to explore all our opportunities, capitalize on them when we can, and increase our financial security.

Make a list of the potential options for using your home to generate additional income. One thing to take into consideration is that just like any rental home there may be times of vacancy, so use an amount that safely takes that into consideration.

Home Income Generation	
Potential Income-Generating Option	Potential Monthly Income
1. _____	$ _____
2. _____	$ _____
3. _____	$ _____
4. _____	$ _____
5. _____	$ _____
Total Potential Additional Income	$ _____

If you are only marginally out of bounds on your housing costs, this next section may help you find a solution by increasing your income to a level that makes them work.

I would never advise someone to try to make a "perfect" plan. No matter how hard you try, you will likely find it still has flaws. Worse yet, spending too much time focusing on the planning phase may cause you to lose your drive to do anything because your life is no longer fun. So just use these tools and strategies to a reasonable extent to compile your ultimate plan. The most important aspect of any successful plan is that it adequately provides constant and safe wealth creation and that it has the potential to get you to your goal.

If you are starting in the hole, the next few years may very well be the hardest. One thing I can assure you of is that not taking action soon will only result in the hardship being longer and more painful later on. Not only that, but if you delay you are shrinking your productive wealth building years which could greatly minimize your retirement lifestyle, or worse—eliminate your ability to retire altogether.

Once you have a surplus it's not as important what you do with the excess. Obviously, I would certainly advise you to spend and invest it wisely on things that make good financial sense, but at that point it will not be nearly as important what you do with it.

NOTES:

_____

_____

_____

_____

_____

_____

_____

_____

_____

_____

_____

REBALANCE BLUEPRINT

Wow! You made it through the hard work of finding out where you currently stand and what options you have for transitioning to a wealth builder. Hopefully you also created a great career improvement plan. Now we're going to get this abundance of information boiled down to a clear plan for transitioning to a Wealth Builder Lifestyle.

You need to create a simple image in your mind of exactly what you need to do to succeed. That image will represent a simple action plan that you will be able to follow daily with very little effort or thought, this will turn your goals into reality. You also need to have a "story" that you can articulate fluently which will serve as your wealth builder rebalance philosophy. It will represent the strategies you will be using to make your transition. The reason why you're doing this is because if you can't visualize and articulate your goals, you are far less likely to achieve them. When you can consciously see it and speak it while you are living it, your subconscious will go to work engraining your actions as your new habits. Whether they realize it or not, everyone who achieves millionaire status has good key habits that support their wealth building lifestyle.

Setting simple boundaries is a powerful tool. For instance, if you say, "I will not spend over $50 a month on entertainment," then you instantly know that going to a $75 concert is out. You don't need to think through or specifically rule out certain ideas because your $50 boundary does that for you, and the only thing you have to focus on is that simple boundary. This is an arbitrary example, but it should help you understand the power of the principle behind this concept.

Security Cushion

Enter your weekly security cushion distributions in the form below. This will give you a clear snapshot of your security cushion plan for the Twelve-Month Rebalance. You can find the monthly contribution total you previously determined on page 110 and then just determine the weeks or pay periods when you will have the money available to make the contributions.

Security Cushion (Twelve-Month Rebalance)		
Weekly Contributions	**Amount**	**Twelve Month Formula**
Week One	$_____	Total Monthly Contribution
Week Two	$_____	×
Week Three	$_____	12
Week Four	$_____	=
Total Monthly Contribution $_____		**Twelve-Month Goal** $_____

Spending Reductions

Enter your finalized personal and necessity spending cuts. These will be your new boundaries of things not to spend on. If you are reducing your budget by one latte a day, for example, put it on the list as well as a plan for how you will achieve it. For the best results, don't leave a void: if you cut a latte, replace it with a free or less expensive alternative such as walking for fifteen minutes. If you don't fill that void, you will likely get sucked back into your old behavior by the vacuum created as a result of eliminating something.

REBALANCE BLUEPRINT

Enter your reductions below, keep your answers short and memorable. Your previously determined list of cuts can be found on pages 117 and 119.

Spending Reductions (Twelve-Month Rebalance)	
Necessity Expense / Action Required	Monthly Total
1. _____ / _____	$ _____
2. _____ / _____	$ _____
3. _____ / _____	$ _____
4. _____ / _____	$ _____
5. _____ / _____	$ _____
6. _____ / _____	$ _____
7. _____ / _____	$ _____
8. _____ / _____	$ _____
9. _____ / _____	$ _____
10. _____ / _____	$ _____
Personal Expense / Action Required	Monthly Total
1. _____ / _____	$ _____
2. _____ / _____	$ _____
3. _____ / _____	$ _____
4. _____ / _____	$ _____
5. _____ / _____	$ _____
6. _____ / _____	$ _____
7. _____ / _____	$ _____
8. _____ / _____	$ _____
9. _____ / _____	$ _____
10. _____ / _____	$ _____
Combined Total of Cuts	$ _____

Debt Reduction

Use the debt reduction hit list information you created from page 128 below.

Hit List (Hit Amount $ _____)						
Creditor	Loan Balance	Minimum Payment	Hit List Payment	Hit Start Date	Payoff Date	APR
_____	$_____	$_____	$_____	_____	_____	___
_____	$_____	$_____	$_____	_____	_____	___
_____	$_____	$_____	$_____	_____	_____	___
_____	$_____	$_____	$_____	_____	_____	___
_____	$_____	$_____	$_____	_____	_____	___
_____	$_____	$_____	$_____	_____	_____	___
_____	$_____	$_____	$_____	_____	_____	___
_____	$_____	$_____	$_____	_____	_____	___
_____	$_____	$_____	$_____	_____	_____	___
_____	$_____	$_____	$_____	_____	_____	___
_____	$_____	$_____	$_____	_____	_____	___
Initial Loan Total $_____			Yearend Balance		$_____	

NOTES :

_____

_____

_____

_____

_____

Rebalance Investment Plan

You should have come up with an amount that you have available each month to put towards investments. Use the amount you came up with from page 124 in the next worksheet. Keep in mind, this wealth building system is not an investment guide with specific recommendations because investment opportunities are constantly changing and you really need to research them for yourself. Don't let that discourage you, you can do it!

For each investment type, you have already determined an allocation amount based on the program guidelines. The number one thing to remember to do is **invest**! There are numerous investment vehicles and yes, some will perform better than others. You may not pick the "best" one, but that's ok. I'm not telling you to purposely lose money—that's obviously not our goal—but if you don't invest, the result will be equal to losing on every investment. If you don't invest you will likely be right where you are now in twenty years, and then it will be too late.

It's not nearly as complicated or scary to figure this stuff out as you may think. Such emotions probably exist simply because you have never done it. Wealth builders don't start out financially savvy. It's a learning process that you too can learn. There are great books out there and the internet gives you lots of options for researching anything you may have questions about. These days, learning the basics and getting started with investing is very simple. Because of all the user friendly investment guides available, you do not need to become a financial genius to make money on investments.

If you're not sure yet which specific investments you're going to use for each category, that's fine, just list the investment amount for each category. Then, at least track and put your investment funds into a savings account so you can get started on your rebalance right away. When you are ready, apply it towards the appropriate investment. Use the following rebalancing guidelines until you can fully meet your standard program guideline percentages.

Investment Allocations (Twelve-Month Rebalance)						
Investment Category	Total Investment Contribution		Rebalance Guideline		Category Contribution	
Security		×	40%	=	$	
Growth	$	×	30%	=	$	
Business		×	30%	=	$	

By completing these forms you will be getting more familiar with where the money's at and should be able to crosscheck all your answers (i.e. the monthly total investments above should equal your monthly total below). If you find a mistake, just go back and see where you went wrong.

Determine the week of the month that specifically corresponds to when you will be making your investment contributions. This will vary based on which pay period or week of the month the allocated amount will be available to you.

Investment Distributions (Twelve-Month Rebalance)					
Investment Category	Week One	Week Two	Week Three	Week Four	Monthly Total
Security	$	$	$	$	$
Growth	$	$	$	$	$
Business	$	$	$	$	$
Totals	$	$	$	$	$

Career Fast-Tracking

Although you will use the action tree created in the career section for specific progress tracking of your goal, list the key steps below to create an overview of the actions required to make your change. For example: Step 1, apply for student loans in next 30 days; Step 2, enroll in trade school within sixty days; and Step 3, search for the best possible position in your new field of work to start building experience. Use as few or many steps as you need. Remember, this is just a broad overview.

Step 1: _____

_____

Step 2: _____

_____

Step 3: _____

_____

Step 4: _____

_____

Step 5: _____

_____

Step 6: _____

_____

Step 7: _____

_____

Step 8: _____

_____

Step 9: _____

_____

Step 10: _____

_____

PART TWO: TWELVE MONTH REBALANCE

This Action Tree will help you plan, track, and monitor progress on your goal. It should contain the same information you previously entered on page 183. If you don't want to re-fill it in here, you can cut out your original one or download and print out a separate Rebalance Blueprint to create your plan.

Career Goal Action Tree			
Goal _____			
STEP	**Progress Tracker** shade one box for every action completed	☐ ☐ ☐ ☐ ☐ ☐ ☐ ☐ ☐	
	Plant the Seed – Write one action that will turn an idea into a real decision.		
1	Your Seed Action	_____	☐
	Set the Roots – Take two power actions that will further commit you to your goal.		
2	First Influential, Root-Setting Action	1. _____	☐
	Second Influential, Root-Setting Action	2. _____	☐
	Accelerate Growth – Take two more power actions that will produce massive growth.		
3	First Influential Fertilization Action	1. _____	☐
	Second Influential Fertilization Action	2. _____	☐
	Shape Your Results – Take two more power actions to fill voids and refine your approach.		
4	First Influential Shaping Action	1. _____	☐
	Second Influential Shaping Action	2. _____	☐
	Perfect Your Outcome – Take two more power actions that clean up any remaining mess.		
5	First Influential Clean-Up Action	1. _____	☐
	Second Influential Clean-Up Action	2. _____	☐

Check the appropriate box after each action is completed.

214

Rebalance Housing Plan

Based on what you read earlier in the rental and housing section, what have you decided?

□ No change   □ Changes per the following plan

In the simplest and most direct way, describe the changes you will make. Then list the action steps you need to take (including the trigger dates or dollar amounts required for such changes). For example: Step 1, immediately start saving $200 for each of the next 6 months; Step 2, in 5 months start looking for a new apartment; and Step 3, in one year (on __/__/____) I will move to a cheaper apartment.

I will make the following change to my housing situation:

_____

_____

In order to successfully complete this change, I will take the following steps when the step trigger is reached:

Step 1: _____

Trigger: _____

Step 2: _____

Trigger: _____

Step 3: _____

Trigger: _____

Step 4: _____

Trigger: _____

Step 5: _____

Trigger: _____

End of Year Goals

Cutting and reducing things is never fun and goes against our need to grow. You want to realign your focus to the future pleasure that will be created by taking these actions, and one of the best ways to do that is to have a clear picture of your goals. I don't mean a physical picture (although that helps), I mean a picture in your mind that you can focus on. Essentially, I'm talking about a snapshot of the outcome you seek and the pleasure associated with it.

You need to be aware of the cuts and changes you need to make to achieve your goals, but your focus should primarily be on the positives. For example, your growing bank account, increasing investments, more security (thanks to your fully-funded cushion), and your net worth being on the rise should all be great consequences of your efforts. Take a few minutes here to visualize your end goals. You can ask yourself the following questions to help inspire your vision.

What would the home you live in look like?

What kind of cars would you drive?

What would you be doing to earn income?

How many hours a week would you work?

What would your coworkers be like?

Are you the boss or a key player?

What would your bank statement look like each month?

What toys would you have (boat, motorcycle, cars, etc.)?

What lifestyle would you be able to provide for your kids?

How would your friends and family view you?

What would you be able to do to contribute and give back?

These are just a few examples of questions you might ask yourself to stimulate your mind's thought processes. It may be helpful to create a list of your own questions that specifically apply to you that will hopefully trigger thoughts about your most important priorities.

Goal Vision Board

A physical image can also help you reflect on and support your mental one. Taking a little time to create a physical snapshot of your outcomes/goals can help support the burning of your goals into your conscious (and ultimately subconscious) mind. A goal vision board can be a handy tool for helping to keep you focused.

A goal vision board is a simple collage of pictures or symbols that represent the goals you wish to achieve. To make one, pick up some type of backing such as poster or foam board which is available at any office supply or box store. It should be of a size that comfortably fits where you plan to keep it. You will want the board in a place where you will see it often. Cut out pictures, text snippets, or other symbols that represent your goals, outcomes, and desires. Attach them to your board in a collage, then every time you see it, take a moment to look it over and think about your action plan for making your goals a reality.

NOTES :

_____

_____

_____

_____

_____

_____

_____

_____

_____

PART TWO: TWELVE MONTH REBALANCE

Use the following form to help estimate your net wealth at the end of your twelve month rebalance. Use a compound interest calculator (such as the one available at http://www.interestcalc.org) to estimate your ending investment values.

Net Wealth Evaluator (Twelve-Month Rebalance)		
(what you own)	**(what you owe)**	
Liquid Assets	**Unsecured Debt**	
Security Cushion $_____	Credit Cards $_____	
Cash, Other $_____	Other Loans $_____	
Total Liquid Assets $_____	**Total Unsecured Debts** $_____	
Real Property Assets	**Real Property Liabilities**	
Primary Residence $_____	Primary Residence $_____	
Other Real Estate $_____	Other Real Estate $_____	
Planes, Boats, RVs $_____	Planes, Boats, RVs $_____	
Automobiles, Motorcycles $_____	Automobiles, Motorcycles $_____	
Personal Property $_____	Other $_____	
Other $_____	Other $_____	
Total Property Assets $_____	**Total Property Liabilities** $_____	
Investment Assets (anticipated end values)	**Total All Liabilities** $_____	
Security Investments $_____	**Rebalance Total Net Wealth**	
Growth Investments $_____	Total (all assets) $_____	
Business Investments $_____	Total (all liabilities) $_____	
Total Investment Assets $_____	**Net Wealth** $_____	
Total All Assets $_____	(net wealth = assets – liabilities)	

"It's not where you start in life that matters, it's where you end up!"

- Daniel Hartjoy

Visual Progress Tracker

Use the following visual progress tracker to enter your current standings and your future goals. Shade in the progress meters as you move closer to each goal. Think of this like a goal dashboard that measures your progress towards each achievement. Following are specific instructions for each of the six categories you will be tracking.

Security Cushion – For your Goal, enter the difference between where you are now and your One-Year Goal, which is the total amount you are looking to grow your cushion by. Divide the difference by twelve and enter the Monthly Goal amount you need to contribute to reach this goal. Shade one cell for each time you save the equivalent of your monthly goal. If you save only half of it one month, for example, shade half a cell.

Spending Reduction – For your Monthly Goal, enter your current spending budget. For your Spending Reduction Goal, subtract your current spending from your Monthly Goal. Then for your One-Year Goal, multiply your Spending Reduction Goal by twelve. Shade one cell for each time you reduce your spending the equivalent of your monthly goal. If you reduce it by only half for one month, for example, shade half a cell.

Investments Goal – For your One-Year Goal, enter the investment balance you wish to have at the end of the year. For your Investments Goal, enter the difference between your current investment balance and your One-Year Goal. Then for your Monthly Goal, divide your Investment Goal by twelve. Shade one cell for each time you invest the equivalent of your monthly goal.

Debt Reduction – For your Debt Reduction Goal, enter the difference between where you are now and your One-Year Goal. Your One-Year Goal should be the ending balance from your Debt Reduction Hit List. Divide the difference by twelve and enter the amount as your Monthly Goal. Shade one cell for each time you pay off the equivalent of your Monthly Goal.

PART TWO: TWELVE MONTH REBALANCE

Career Income – For your Career Income Increase, subtract your Current Income from your Target Income and enter that amount. There are ten boxes, each one of which represents 10% of your career increase. If you get a pay increase that gets you 40% of the way there, for example, shade four cells.

Housing Cost – For your Housing Cost Decrease, subtract your Current Cost from your Goal Cost and enter the amount you need to decrease this expense by. As you complete each of the three steps you decided were necessary to successfully achieve this reduction, shade in one cell.

NOTES :

_____

_____

_____

_____

_____

_____

_____

_____

_____

_____

_____

_____

_____

REBALANCE BLUEPRINT

Visual Progress Tracker			

Progress		Progress	
	$_____ One-Year Goal		$_____ One-Year Goal
	Security Cushion		**Spending Reduction**
	Goal ↑ $_____		Goal ↓ $_____
	$_____ Monthly Goal		$_____ Monthly Goal

Progress		Progress	
	$_____ One-Year Goal		$_____ One-Year Goal
	Investments		**Debt Reduction**
	Goal ↑ $_____		Goal ↓ $_____
	$_____ Monthly Goal		$_____ Monthly Goal

Progress		Progress		
	$_____ Target Income	Step Three	$_____ Goal Cost
	Career Income	Step Two	**Housing Cost**
	Increase ↑ $_____		Decrease ↓ $_____
	$_____ Current Income	Step One	$_____ Current Cost

Current Net Worth $_____   Target Net Worth $_____

Net Worth Goal Progress: ☐ ☐ ☐ ☐ ☐ ☐ ☐ ☐ ☐ ☐

Net Worth Increase Goal $_____

Income Distribution Plan

Use this form to create your monthly income distribution action plan. You may need to update this along the way should your income increase or decrease. Use this every time you get paid to simplify your distributions and ensure you are following your rebalance blueprint.

Income Distribution Plan (Twelve-Month Rebalance)

Weekly Income		Distribution Category and Payment Destinations						
	Week Number	Cushion (savings)	Housing (checking)	Necessities (checking)	Personal (checking and cash)	Investments (direct deposit)	Fun Money (cash)	Hit List (pay vendor)
Total Income		$ _____	$ _____	$ _____	$ _____	$ _____	$ _____	$ _____
	1	$ _____	$ _____	$ _____	$ _____	$ _____	$ _____	$ _____
	2	$ _____	$ _____	$ _____	$ _____	$ _____	$ _____	$ _____
	3	$ _____	$ _____	$ _____	$ _____	$ _____	$ _____	$ _____
	4	$ _____	$ _____	$ _____	$ _____	$ _____	$ _____	$ _____
Income Monthly Total $ _____		Cushion Monthly Total $ _____	Housing Monthly Total $ _____	Necessities Monthly Total $ _____	Personal Monthly Total $ _____	Investments Monthly Total $ _____	Fun Money Monthly Total $ _____	Debt Monthly Total $ _____

Maximizing Your Results

Now that you have created an action plan to transition in to a Wealth Builder Lifestyle, where do you go from here? As you live your new lifestyle you will constantly be tested and have to make numerous financial decisions, some small, some major, but they will all have an impact on your wealth building success. In Part Three we are going to look at eleven essential wealth builder strategies and decision making tools that will support your wealth building efforts.

By using these eleven wealth builder essentials, you will create an environment that will foster financial success. Incorporating the following characteristics into your lifestyle as well as using the appropriate tools when applicable will help maximize the results you get from living a Wealth Builder Lifestyle.

NOTES :

_____

_____

_____

_____

_____

_____

_____

_____

_____

_____

PART THREE: WEALTH BUILDER ESSENTIALS

INVESTING 101

Investing is one of the most prevalent difference between those who are rich (or becoming rich) and those who are not. If you want to get on track for the former, start investing now regardless of how much or what the method involves. Just start investing.

That may sound like reckless financial advice, but if you are not already investing, you likely have little to no money set aside working to build wealth for you. Furthermore, if you look five years into your past you probably had the same amount saved or invested as you do right now. And if you make no change, five years from now you will *still* have the same. So no matter the circumstances, just start consistently investing even a small amount now.

Sure, if you put no effort in to making at least a semi-informed investment, you may lose 100% of it. That wouldn't be good, but as long as you make reasonable efforts to avoid that when making your decisions, that's not very likely. Worst-case scenario, you would only end up where you currently are today. The risk of not making forward progress is far higher when you choose not to invest at all. Don't let the fear of not being a good investor or of potentially taking a loss chain you to a life of servitude.

There are three investment categories that the Wealth Builder Lifestyle promotes, and I'll share some of the vehicles you may want to use for each of these categories. You should never put all your money in to any one investment, especially not a high-risk, high-growth one. That's a fool's idea of smart! Don't let your emotions get the best of you when you see the possibilities.

I am not a certified investment advisor, so keep in mind that these concepts are my opinions only and may not be right for you. That being said, these investment strategies have been used very successfully by some of the best know wealth builders. If you choose to invest in anything that you are not fully competent in, you should seek out the required training to get educated and be up to speed so that you can make informed decisions. You can take classes, hire an advisor, or do research on your own, but ultimately any investment decisions are your sole responsibility. I'll end with one last caveat: there are some good financial experts and some bad ones, so either way you go you really need to do your own homework to fully understand any deals you are going to make.

Security Investments

These can be things like cash, precious metals, your home, and low-risk growth mutual funds. Your goal is to average a 7% annual return with very minimal risk.

Growth Investments

My preferences here include mutual funds in the following three categories: growth and income, aggressive growth, and international. These are not the only options, but keep in mind that your primary goal here is to get a return in excess of 10% without substantial risk.

Business Investments

Some options for this investment class are purchasing aggressive growth mutual funds, directly funding someone else's business, or investing in a business of your own. Your goal is to generate a return in excess of 15%, and to do this you are likely going to have to take on more risk. That is why these are called *business* investments. No business can guarantee profit, but that's why they have the potential to generate higher than normal returns.

I'm a skeptic of "expert" advice when it comes to investments, and you should be too. There is no shame in applying a healthy dose of skepticism when interacting with anyone doling out financial advice. When it comes to my money, I'm the only expert I trust. I go out of my way to get the best possible information from the best possible sources when evaluating whether something is truly worthy of my financial investment.

Throughout the recent financial crisis, I watched the majority of the talking heads and so-called experts on TV give out some of the worst advice of the 21st century. This advice surely lead to substantial financial losses for anyone that followed it.

I advise you to read books or take training courses by qualified experts as you get started. You don't have to be an expert yourself, but growing your expertise over time will help you be a more competent and successful investor. Eventually this will also help you keep any financial experts you hire in check.

Following are five things I think you should consider when trying to find a financial expert to represent your interest.

Credentials

If someone claims to be a financial expert, they had better be able to support their claim. Not only that, but there are varying degrees in this category: CPAs, RIAs, CFPs, CFAs, and all kinds of other acronyms. The term financial expert is used loosely, but includes many levels of expertise and specialty. As a comparison, just because someone has expert training in the medical field doesn't mean they are qualified to do open heart surgery.

Where's the Money?

Financial advisors do what they do for a reason: to make money. There's nothing wrong with them making money, but you need to know where and how they will be making it off of you so you can evaluate their investment approach. If they are a fiduciary, they have to place their client's best interests ahead of their own and disclose how they are compensated. Although their obligation to make you aware of how they are compensated is good, I'm not necessarily saying a fiduciary is the way to go. After all, such a decision may actually limit your wealth building potential due to the reduced number of services they may be able to offer. The main thing is to evaluate their motivations for recommending certain investments. Don't be afraid to ask. It's your money and only you will truly look to protect it.

Cost

This may seem like the same thing we just covered, but it is different. The above question was primed at determining any background sources of income they might generate from directing your money into certain assets. The intention of this concern, however, is to understand how much you can anticipate their services costing you directly. This is important information for determining the total potential upside of working with them. Take for instance a $10,000 investment you make with a firm that historically returns around 13% per year. A $1,300 return on your investment isn't bad. On the other hand, if they are charging you a 5% management fee for handling the investment it will affect your overall return. In this case, the management cost would be $500. To calculate your real potential return, you need to subtract the fees ($500) from your return ($1,300). So the actual potential return of such an investment would be 8% or $800, which really isn't that great. Do your homework up front so you are not surprised later.

Track Record

Just like a pie-in-the-sky forecast, goals and expectations are all great but history is the most accurate predictor of the future. Find out what their historical returns have been, including proof for any investments they are pushing. Make sure the performance is not just for a one-year period (everyone gets a homerun every once in a while). I would look for at least a five-year track record that represents the results you want. Don't just ask once. If the advisor you choose suggests another investment instrument or approach, ask to see the five-year track record before agreeing to make the move. You can minimize your risk with proven results.

Fit and Strategy

It's not "one size fits all" when seeking the best fit for your goal and interest representation. This most often comes down to the strategy or approach of the financial expert or service. Some may represent large-dollar investors with several million invested (and therefore make them a priority), to whom you may seem like small potatoes. You're not likely to get the personal attention you want with a company like that. Or, you just may not relate to how they dress, act, and talk—they may be used to servicing a certain type of client that doesn't match who you are. If you're a new investor, you may want a smaller firm that can take the time to give you some personal attention and help you understand what it takes to get started. A company that will take the time to make sure your investment growth strategy is in line with your wealth-building plan is crucial. Working with an advisor or company that is a good fit and that provides the services that support your investment strategy can greatly enhance your results and comfort in working together.

Investing Resources

You do not necessarily need to hire an investment firm to make investments or manage your money for you. Those resources may help you feel more comfortable getting started but these days they are not required. With the internet you have access to a world of resources and information that allows anyone the ability to get informed and make their own investments.

The number one thing I hear that stops people from investing is that they just don't know how or where to go. These days, it truly couldn't be any easier. If you have never invested before or have limited investing experience, here are a few places you can go online for more information or to get started. All of these links will take you to online investment companies where you can easily setup an account within minutes. Most have no minimum investment to get started, but there may be one to open your IRAs. If that's the case, just contribute to your equities until you have enough invested to roll it over into an IRA.

These brokerages all provide their own investing resources (such as stock and fund performance histories) so you can easily do related research. Then once you are ready, select the fund or stock you want to buy, how many shares you want, then just click buy. In case you were unaware, stocks and mutual funds are sold in shares. Essentially, they're just tiny pieces of a business. The share cost varies by company, so if you want to buy $500 of a certain company then divide that amount by the individual share price to determine how many shares you should purchase.

TD Ameritrade - https://www.tdameritrade.com

Scottrade - https://www.scottrade.com

Etrade - https://www.etrade.com

Vanguard - https://investor.vanguard.com

The sources listed here are in no particular order. I have no affiliations or ties with any of them, they are just some of the most popular and easy to use options out there. You can also setup your online trading account to automatically transfer a set amount from your checking account each month. This can automate your investment contributions so you can effortlessly stay on track and meet your investing requirements. All of these online trading companies have very good support and instructions, so there is no need to be intimidated. You don't need to have any ninja investor credentials to be successful.

Investment Fund Flow

You want to make sure you fund the most beneficial investments first, so I'm going to present my recommendation. If you have the option of an employer-matched 401K, you will want to max that out first. Then fully max out your Roth and/or Traditional IRAs before rolling into your traditional mutual funds. Here is a little breakdown of why you want to fund in this particular order.

Employer-Matched 401K

This one should be pretty obvious: you make an immediate return on your investment of up to 100% of every dollar you invest, which is pretty hard to beat. Most employers will match up to a certain limit, so if possible you should contribute up to that amount.

Roth IRA

With a Roth IRA, you make post-tax contributions, so you invest out of your net income. The beauty of this is that when you start withdrawing in retirement your withdrawals will be tax-free. As you get closer to retirement, the importance of funding your Roth IRA will diminish because it will have less time to grow (negating the value of net investment dollars). If you do not have at least 15 years (preferably 20) to allow your Roth investment to grow before you touch them, the benefits for most users will be lost or at best a break even. As you get close to this being a consideration talk to your accountant or financial advisor to determine the best time for you to stop contributing to this investment tool.

Traditional IRA

Your contributions may be tax deductible; meaning the money you contribute would not be subject to income taxes. This means that what you would normally have to pay in income tax you could actually invest and earn interest on. However, when you finally make withdrawals at retirement, they will be taxed as income.

Both IRAs

Many people will qualify for both IRA types, which have maximum annual contribution limits. They both have rules for early withdrawals, and in addition, a traditional IRA (currently) has mandatory distribution requirements beginning at the age of 70½. The reason you want to fund IRAs first is because you can still invest in similar instruments (like mutual funds), but the tax benefits make IRAs more attractive than just straight equity investments. So max them out if you can!

Traditional Mutual Funds

Invest in these last since they do not have matching or tax incentives. That doesn't make them bad, just not as great!

Keep the following flow chart below in mind when you are thinking about which investments to contribute to first.

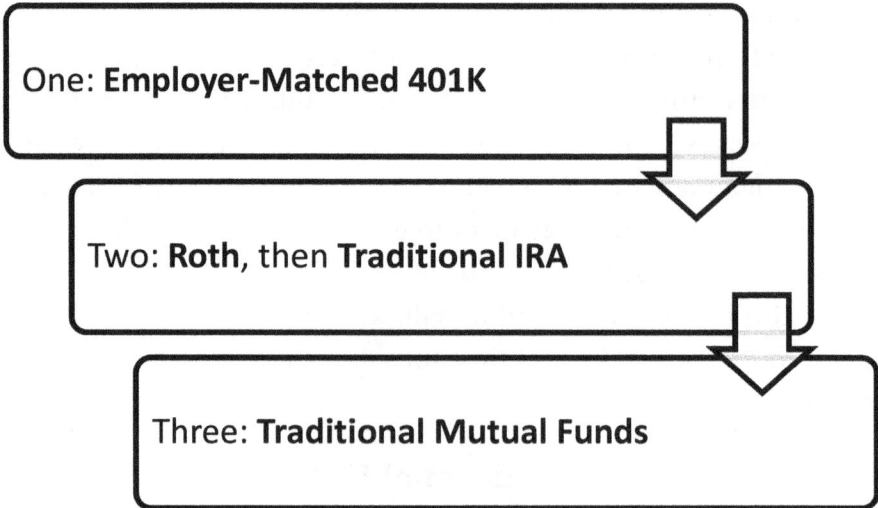

One: **Employer-Matched 401K**

Two: **Roth**, then **Traditional IRA**

Three: **Traditional Mutual Funds**

Cash Flow Assets

Cash flow assets include (by definition) any asset that you invest in that increases your monthly or yearly income. Some assets (like your home) do not necessarily contribute to your cash flow but instead may increase your net worth. Focusing at least some of your investment money on assets that increase your monthly or at least yearly income in a way that is liquid builds financial strength. This will put you in a better position in the event of an income disruption or loss as you will have additional income sources.

A few options for cash flow assets are:

1. Income-producing rental properties
2. Stocks that pay dividends
3. Loans that receive interest-only payments until they are due in full

The last option is unique, but might be available when lending money to a business so they can cover their operating expenses until a particular receivable comes in.

There are some great books out there almost exclusively on the topic of cash flow investments. In particular, Robert Kyosaki has a few great resources in his Rich Dad series of books.

Always remember to stay diversified, don't get overleveraged, and consistently work at building your net worth. I don't support the approach of any "financial guru" that pushes people to get too close to the edge in an attempt to get rich. Those strategies can take all the progress from years of good wealth building efforts and quickly destroy everything you have been working for. That type of extreme wealth destruction comes from a get-rich-quick mentality that is overly greedy and money centric.

Money – A Silent Employee

The way I look at *every* dollar is that each has the potential to be a hassle-free, silent employee. If you don't want to own a business I can totally understand, but I still think we all need something consistently working for us to build wealth. Investments give us the opportunity to leverage something small today that will grow and mature into something much greater later on in life. Every time you spend a dollar, think of that action as permanently firing one of your potential employees. That employee would have been more than happy to work and build wealth for you for a lifetime without complaint.

If you haven't already gotten excited about investing or at least come to the conclusion that you need to and should be consistently investing over the long term, take a look at these little facts. You are likely over 18, but I want you to see the real power of investing. If you put away just $1 at age 18 into an investment that averages a 12% annual return, when you retire at 65 that one dollar will be worth $205 dollars. So say instead of moving out you live at home with your parents for one extra year and work a job—any job, even one for minimum wage. Then you contribute $430 a month over the next twelve months (a grand total of $5,160) to an investment with an anticipated 12% annual return. At the age of 19, your net worth would probably exceed 99% of your peers', and even if you never invested another cent, by the time you reach age 65 you could be a millionaire.

This is absolutely possible due to the power of compound interest (which we will cover more in the next section) but before I move on let's look at one more scenario. Let's say when your kid is born you invest $1,000 one time into an investment account returning 12%. If you contribute nothing else, by the time your child is ready to head out to college you will end up with an investment amount of about $7,690. Not bad—after all, your investment did increase by almost 8 times its original worth. Now, let's say you are a strict parent trying to instill a good work ethic in your child by making them find their own way to pay for college. Instead of pulling that money out, you just leave that money to sit in a trust until they retire at 65. That one-time $1,000 investment would end up being worth $1,582,000.

Why with all this opportunity in the world are so many people retiring broke? It's because they either don't take the time to get even a basic financial education or they procrastinate and don't take the necessary actions. It's never too late. If you haven't started, look at the potential in these opportunities and get started today. Furthermore, if you are a parent or will be a parent you need to teach your kids about wealth building while they are young. Do your kids a favor and don't send them out into the world foolishly unprepared when I just showed you two simple ways that you can help make sure your kids retire millionaires. The most expensive of those options would only cost you

$1,000, and I know your kids are worth it to you so take some action. Although, I guess in one of those scenarios you would have to keep them around for an extra year... Ah, suck it up, it's worth it!

The Compound Effect

We've briefly touched on this subject, but now I want to go a little more in-depth on the topic. The compound effect, unfortunately, cuts both ways. So it's important that you have a clear understanding of how it works and how you do or don't want it affecting your life. This concept is the primary reason why savers are losers and investors are winners.

We've all heard about inflation. It usually averages a few percent each year, around 2% to 4% annually. Savers and investors both need to keep this in mind, but the former need to even more so since they don't have any protection against inflation. This is one of the reasons why a home is more of a security investment rather than a growth investment. Historically (outside of boom markets, which always bust), home values tend to barely outpace inflation—if at all—which is really the way it should be.

You really need to focus on and beat the most blatant and unrelenting adverse compound-like effect that plagues us all: inflation. It may seem like 2 to 4% is a pretty small and harmless number unless you recognize it for what it truly is (an exponentially increasing rate). If it didn't increase at an exponential rate, that 3% average annual rise over thirty years would equate to a cost increase of 90% (30 × 3%). So that loaf of bread that cost $1 thirty years ago would only cost $1.90 now. Sadly, that's not how it works. A 3% inflation rate over thirty years actually amounts to an increase of 143% ($1.03^{30}-1.0$), so now your bread actually costs $2.43. Therefore, if you go the savings route, the dollar you save now will not even get you half of a loaf in thirty years. If, on the other hand, you invest in a 3% CD you will have protection against inflation and you will still be able to buy a full loaf come that time.

PART THREE: WEALTH BUILDER ESSENTIALS

Figure out at what age you want to retire (for example, 65). Then subtract that from your estimated life expectancy (85 in our example case). I came up with 20 years, but of course your answer may differ. Then, multiply the lowest amount you could get by on right now by the number of years your last calculation came to (20 for me). We will assume that a reasonable annual living equals $24,000, or $2,000 a month. This example also assumes you are thirty years from retirement.

Example:

	Step 1:	85	-	65	=	20 years
	Step 2:	20	×	$24,000	=	$480,000

Your numbers:

Step 1: _____ - _____ = _____

Step 2: _____ × _____ = _____

That's the amount you would need to save for retirement if there was no inflation. Now, let's assume our inflation rate of 3% is accurate so I can give you an idea of how much you will *really* need to save.

Example:

Desired annual allowance: **$24,000**

Years until retirement: **30**

Total required (no inflation): **$480,000**

Total required on retirement day (based on a 3% inflation rate): **$1,165,000**

Yikes! Inflation is insane, is it not? This calculation is just accounting for the inflation that will occur between now and when our example retires (in our case, 30 years). Unfortunately, it doesn't stop there.

Not only do we have to account for those extra years, but due to inflation's compound-like nature the numbers get dramatically

238

worse much quicker. You may find it hard to believe, but that's the actual amount someone in the example situation would have to save to be able to retire at their current standard of living. Unfortunately, the math on that one is relatively complex (thanks to the compound effect), so there is no simple equation for me to share with you that would allow you to perform your own specific calculation.

So, based on our example you would have to save $52,200 per year for 30 years to save for a retirement equal to your current standard of living. I'm going to make a wild assumption here and say that most people with a baseline of $24,000 do not have the ability to save $52,200 a year for retirement, which is exactly why savers are losers in the long run.

Now, just for kicks let's look at a simple counter-example using the compound effect in our favor by investing. You would only need to invest $510 a month ($6,120 a year) for 30 years into an investment account earning a 12% return to exceed that $1,566,000. That is the amount you would have when you reached the age of 65. Sounds pretty nice, right? Well hold on, it gets much better! You could pull an annual income of nearly $200,000 off of that investment without touching a single penny of your $1.6 million principal!

Your desired $24,000 retirement lifestyle would be costing you an inflation-adjusted $81,600, so you would have exceeded your goal by over double while only investing $183,600. Not only that, but when you die you will still be a millionaire. Even if you had miraculously saved the amount you needed instead of going the investment route, you would still die broke at 85. Moreover, if you did happen to live longer, you would have a serious financial problem.

The important part here is to just start investing, don't chance it or assume you can save your way to a great retirement. The first step is the hardest, but once you start investing you will quickly get more familiar with how these things work. Soon you will see just how simple it is to invest and grow your money and wonder why you ever feared you couldn't do it.

I encourage you to accept the notion that you can't possibly save enough money to retire. Even if you could save up the amount you needed, it would be foolish to let inflation constantly erode your wealth while your money is just sitting. If you take the few simple steps required to invest your money, not only will it grow to offset the negative effects of inflation, it will generate more free wealth you won't have to work for.

"Through your habits you can choose to live the lifestyle of the rich and famous or the poor and destitute. Only you can decide!"

- Daniel Hartjoy

PERSONAL FINANCE IS YOUR BUSINESS

Operate your personal financial life like a business. Your personal financial life must turn a profit so you can afford to sustain the occasional loss. Our lives are governed under the same principles as a business. You can't go through life just breaking even or you'll never move ahead, always teetering on the verge of failure. Businesses have to make a profit for survival, and people also need to be making a profit and putting those profits back to work for them to build a better future and a strong safety net. When someone files bankruptcy, it's typically because they treated their financial life like a poorly-run business with no profit, no reinvestment, and no security cushion.

In the past, we have seen some big corporations bringing in $500 million dollar profits and consequently being looked down upon by the public under the premise of being greedy. But the sad truth is that those critics rarely realize that the business's profits are relative to its size, a burden that means they may have to shoulder losses that are every bit as impressive. These titans may take $75 million dollar losses quarterly, and if not for those seemingly huge profits, these companies would go bankrupt and leave their employees out of work. Those are harsh consequences for everyone involved, and they are just as harsh for us individually when we manage our personal affairs poorly.

Do yourself a big favor and don't live on the edge of financial ruin. Structure your financial life to consistently earn a profit and then re-invest to build a rock-solid financial future of security and prosperity.

Financial Peace of Mind

Don't forget your security cushion. It may not seem like a great wealth building tool as the compound-like effects of inflation work against it, but it's your insurance policy against the rough patches you **will** eventually have.

When you know you are consistently building wealth and have a nice chunk of cash sitting in your bank account, you will feel financially strong and secure. Just think for a moment of how you would feel with twelve months' worth of your living expenses sitting in the reserve. How would you feel knowing that if you lost your job, got injured, or had some other unexpected expense come up that you could cover it without having to sell off your assets, run up your credit cards, or stress about how you are going to get by? *That* is truly having peace of mind.

NOTES :

_____

_____

_____

_____

_____

_____

_____

_____

_____

_____

FINANCIAL FENG SHUI: YOUR ENVIRONMENT

Some of the most powerful and easy to harness forces that can help get you moving in the Wealth Builder Lifestyle are in your surrounding environment. These natural forces are continually working for or against you without any conscious effort on your part. It's important to take some steps to make sure you are living primarily in environments that are pushing and pulling you in a positive direction. You also need to try to minimize any counterproductive environmental forces.

Personal Associations

One of the most powerful types of environmental forces are your personal relationships. Consider that you are best represented by the average of the five people you spend the most time around. Right now, we are specifically talking about your wealth, so look at the wealth status of those people. Are their financial statuses reminiscent of the results you are after? Are their net worth, debt, and income values in line with what you hope to achieve? Are they living lifestyles that continually increase their level of wealth?

If you can't answer yes to these three questions, you need to come up with a plan to realign your key personal associations. This one change can help get you moving in the right direction. I'm not saying you have to isolate yourself from your friends, family, or other important people in your life. What I'm saying is that it can be very beneficial to spend less time with people that don't represent what you want out of life and more time with those that do.

In the following space, make a list of the five people that represent lifestyles you *don't* want to gravitate towards. You should reduce or even consider eliminating your time with these acquaintances (if they are not positively influencing your life).

Five people I need to limit exposure to or cut associations with completely:

1. _____

2. _____

3. _____

4. _____

5. _____

Now list the five people that you want to build relationships with or focus on spending more time with. If you can't come up with that many, expand your friend base.

Five people I need to include in my key group of associations:

1. _____

2. _____

3. _____

4. _____

5. _____

Don't underestimate the power of good associations. They will pull you effortlessly in their direction—whether good or bad—so make sure their direction is ultimately aligned with the one you desire.

Physical Associations

Next, you need to look at your physical environment. Most people choose things like where you live, work, dine, go for recreation, and so on based on things other than their financial goals. These environmental associations can have a dramatic impact on your fiscal prosperity. Could you imagine an actor aspiring to be a major movie star living in Colorado? How about someone that wants to become a surfing champion living in Alaska? Maybe these people could achieve their dreams, but there would be some major obstacles working against them based solely on their physical location. Examine your life and consider if you may not be in the best physical location to meet your goals.

Your physical environment is not just about where you live. It also includes things like where you spend your time outside your home. For instance, dining in an atmosphere filled with people that are living the lifestyle you seek can help you take on the image of someone similar. This will also put you in an environment to make positive contacts and friends.

Some other great environmental resources for achieving this are seminars, classes, and clubs. If you want to become a real estate investor, taking some classes or attending a seminar can not only provide you with an abundance of knowledge on the subject but also surround you with similar-minded individuals.

If you live in a bad area with high crime or few economic opportunities but can't currently afford to move, making the extra effort to travel outside your neighborhood could pay off big. Performing your work and social interactions in an area that is more prosperous greatly increases your chances of breaking out and creating a better lifestyle for yourself. If someone who has the deck stacked against them just packed up and moved to an area filled with better people and opportunities, odds are they would get caught up in the current of the average standards of that area and have their life changed forever.

Initially, it may be hard to hang out in a more prosperous environment if you don't have the money to rent a place and you don't have any friends there. But if you persevere and hang out there long enough to get a job and acquire a few buddies, you will likely have changed the trajectory of your life as well as that of your following generations. It's hard to stay down when you are surrounded with successful people. Eventually their success will rub off on you.

PART THREE: WEALTH BUILDER ESSENTIALS

Most people that come from a disadvantaged area tend to believe that how they currently live would be the same no matter the location. That belief is probably accompanied by the thought that they could never survive in an area filled with high achievers. Those beliefs create a predetermined fate and are the chains that will bind them, keeping them stuck right where they are. If that's you, I challenge you to discard those beliefs and take action. If you cross the tracks into that new environment, I know you can succeed regardless of the obstacles. Maybe someone you know is shackled by these beliefs, in which case I challenge you to pass this information on and help them break their own chains.

I have personally confronted false beliefs in my life about certain physical locations, careers, and other matters, so I know it is possible to succeed in environments that appear outside of our abilities. It all starts with the boldness to believe you can and that life has more to offer you than what you currently have. Think through how your current physical environments may be limiting you and what changes (big or small) could put you in better ones that will help cultivate your success.

Make a list of five environmental changes you will make that will put you in areas that support your goals and provide opportunities for success (or at least allow you to socialize with people that have achieved the success you desire).

Five changes I will make to my physical environment that supports my new goals:

1. _____

2. _____

3. _____

4. _____

5. _____

FINANCIAL FENG SHUI: YOUR ENVIRONMENT

Sometimes the most powerful thing we can do is keep ourselves out of the environments that support our old habits that have prevented us from succeeding. If your plan involves cutting your costs on discretionary expenses like coffee, don't schedule to meet your friends at your favorite coffee shop. There are other places with comfortable chairs to hang out. What are some strong contributors to your failure to change your bad habits that are working against you?

Five physical environments I will not go to that are keeping me from achieving my goals:

1. _____
2. _____
3. _____
4. _____
5. _____

NOTES :

_____

_____

_____

_____

_____

_____

_____

_____

_____

_____

YOUR IMAGE

Do you have any bad financial habits? Here's an amazing example of how five little habits that most of us have will end up costing us a million dollars in wealth over our lifetime.

A Million Dollars of Bad Habits		
The Bad Habits	Wealth Waster Lifestyle	Wealth Builder Lifestyle
Coffee Budget	$20	$8
Cell Phone	$130	$65
Movie Service	$9	$0
Cable	$75	$0
Dining Out	$30	$0
Total Habit Costs	$264	$73
	Total Monthly Savings	$191

The example above is based on: cutting back one specialty coffee drink per week to just regular coffee; utilizing a pre-paid smart phone instead of the latest trendy device on a contract plan; cutting your internet-based movie service; dropping cable; and reducing your regimen of dining out by one time a month (not eliminating it, just cutting one time).

How will you ever get by without all that cool stuff? Very well, actually! Not only will you set yourself up to have a million dollars when you retire (which will be really awesome), but you will also be cutting unproductive time spent behind a television or computer screen. This will free up more time to do some things that can add real value to your life, like maybe taking a class that will improve your career options.

Now, let's have some fun doing a little math. Let's say we start this cut-back at age 30. We are saving $191 a month, so by the time we are 65 (420 months later) we will have saved **$80,220** (420 × $191).

That's not a million dollars! Wait, there is one more bad habit I forgot to put on the list: **not investing.** We are not going to just save that $191, we are going to contribute it monthly to an income and growth mutual fund with a target return of 12%. By doing so we get some new math that looks like this: 420 × $191 = **$1,053,000.** And there you have it! A million dollars, generated just by changing a few bad habits.

Wealth Building Superstar

Ok, so maybe using the term "superstar" is over-glamorizing a wealth builder's image, but the picture you maintain internally and externally will affect your ability to build wealth. How you see yourself and how others see you helps define the way people interact with you and the opportunities that will be presented to you.

If you are someone that is loose with money and always willing to pick up the tab, you will have many opportunities coming your way to do just that. If, on the other hand, when people go out to lunch with you they know they will have to let go of their own hard-earned money, they likely will not be so eager to go on as many lunch dates (consequently saving you a lot of money). If you are someone that people know is always looking for a good financial opportunity to grow your wealth, you will be amazed at how many prospects will appear seemingly out of nowhere.

If you see yourself as someone that spends too much who will never be able to build wealth, you are not likely to save money or look for investment opportunities simply because of your self-perception. On the other side of that coin, if you see yourself as a penny-pinching power investor you are not going to easily let go of money and you will be continually looking for investment opportunities. Write a brief description of your current wealth builder image. How do you currently view yourself when it comes to wealth building? How do you believe others see you?

YOUR IMAGE

How do you currently feel and think about money and wealth building?

_____

_____

_____

How do others view you in regards to money and wealth building?

_____

_____

_____

Do you think these internal and external images define someone who is destined to be financially successful? Do these descriptions match how you would envision someone you know who is financially successful? Do you believe your current descriptions empower you and support your attempt to build wealth?

Write out descriptions for a new empowering image that supports your desired wealth building goals. How do you need to see yourself? What traits do you need to emanate to those around you? Think about how the people you know who are already successful act and the attitude they display regarding wealth and money. Then think of how you would act and the attitude you would have if you were already a millionaire.

With your new image, how would you feel and think about money and wealth building?

_____

_____

_____

With your new image, how would others view you in regards to money and wealth building?

_____

_____

_____

Your Personal Slogan

Create an empowering, memorable slogan that represents your new wealth builder image. Take into consideration your biggest weaknesses and the things you need to do different. An example for someone that spends too much on little items (that have no long-term value) and has a hard time investing might be, "I'm a powerful wealth building investor with no tolerance for wasteful spending." It can be as long or as short as you want, just keep it simple and easy to remember. You want your slogan to play in your head every time you walk by somewhere that has the potential to suck the wealth building potential right out of you.

My personal wealth builder slogan:

_____

_____

_____

NOTES :

_____

_____

_____

_____

YOUR FOCUS

It is always important to maintain your focus on the things that impact your dreams the most. By this point you should have a pretty clear idea of where you're doing well and where you need the most improvement. Based on your personal situation, determine the three personal keys that are the most important for you to maintain focus on to become a successful wealth builder. Once again, keep them simple and memorable. Essentially, these will be your new operating guidelines.

Things to do More of

These are the items you want to do more of: saving, investing, improving your income, building assets, paying down debt, etc. Write out your new "to-do" list for building wealth.

My personal points to do more of:

1. _____
2. _____
3. _____

Things to Minimize

These are the things you may need to do sometimes, that don't really serve your wealth building lifestyle. Write out your new "to-limit" list for things to keep to a minimum (excessive discretionary spending, unnecessary driving, and so on).

My personal points to minimize:

1. _____
2. _____
3. _____

Things to Eliminate

These are things that destroy or greatly hurt your wealth building potential that should be totally eliminated. Write out your new *never-to-do* list for things to avoid at all costs (use credit cards, take on more debt, and so on).

My personal points to eliminate:

1. _____

2. _____

3. _____

NOTES :

_____

_____

_____

_____

_____

_____

_____

_____

_____

_____

_____

LIVE IN THE MOMENT:
SPEND IN THE PAST OR FUTURE

Most people focus on earning, saving, and investing for wealth building. Although all of those are great actions that almost everyone has the ability to do, many end up outspending their progress. It takes discipline to keep tight reigns on the money and not erode your progress. Unfortunately, training self-restraint is often easier said than done.

So the "live in the moment, spend in the past or future" strategy is meant to cause interference in your spending. Using this strategy can greatly reduce or eliminate your impulse purchases and emotional spending. It also increases the chances you will get the best deals and stretch the dollars you do decide to spend.

So what does it mean to spend in the past or future? Essentially, you will do away with spending in the moment. If you want to go on a vacation, you will not monetize your plans when you decide you want to go. Instead, you will give yourself a cooling off period, a time more commonly spent going through buyer's remorse from poor financial decisions. We don't necessarily need to use discipline to walk away. Instead we can use the distraction of planning to buy us some time to come to our senses and understand the true impact of the decision before pulling the trigger. This is not about making the decision of whether to spend or not to spend, only about creating a delay that gives you the time to make sure your decision supports your lifestyle and goals.

A good decision involves making sure the purchase is in line with your overall plan. You need to make sure you can actually afford it and that you have taken the time to research the best possible deal available. This way, you are sure to get the best value for the money you spend. Maybe you want to take a vacation and it does ultimately turn out to be in line with your plan. Delaying and waiting to spend in the future gives you time to make sure it's well planned, intelligently purchased, and within the financial budget you have allocated.

The result is that you end up not spending "in the moment." You delay awhile and end up spending in the future. When you are on your vacation, you will be enjoying money that you actually spent in the past. There's no instant gratification here. It may just sound like word mumbo jumbo, but it can have a serious effect on your ability to build wealth.

This doesn't mean that you can buy anything you want just because in the past you already considered purchasing it. This means you have to make the decision to buy beforehand and then wait to actually do it. The purchase still needs to fit into your overall financial lifestyle and plan. Essentially, you want to eliminate instant gratification.

Research has shown that there are many great benefits that come from delayed gratification. Even practicing this with your children can be very beneficial to their overall success in life. People that have low impulse control and frequently succumb to needs for instant gratification are far more likely to have high levels of debt, low self-discipline, and an attitude that they don't need to put in effort to get what they want. All of those characteristics are key ingredients for financial and personal underachievement. The good thing is that they can all be changed with a little effort.

Spending for Stimulation

Spending just to obtain stimulation has become an epidemic in our society. Not only do we not want to wait for gratification, but we also have a desire for constant stimulation that we look to gain from expending money. We seek it for enjoyment but the happiness it grants rarely lasts, which leads to a life of continual spending in an attempt to feed an insatiable desire.

LIVE IN THE MOMENT: SPEND IN THE PAST OR FUTURE

Think about all the things you bought and what your motivation for purchasing them was. Was your spending to obtain some short-term stimulation like watching a movie? If so, consider cutting some of that spending by finding new ways to entertain yourself.

This will not only help you save money but can also have substantial rewards like building your creativity skills, of which there has been a dramatic reduction of here in the US. It was creativity and invention that made the US such a remarkable success, and it's the loss of those talents and abilities that will erode the future value of this great nation. Creativity is like a muscle: it needs exercise to get stronger.

In today's modern society we have an abundance of people relying on other people's creativity to provide us with amusement instead of being creative and generating it for ourselves. Consider your stimulation sources throughout a twelve-hour day. Where do they come from? Did you produce them, or were they products created by others such as movies, video games, television shows, YouTube videos, newspapers, amusement parks, alcohol, drugs, and so on?

This may seem a little bit off the topic of building wealth, but being successful in business or a career often hinges on your ability to be creative, ingenuitive, or think outside the box in some other way. This is also an important element in overcoming poor, stimulation-seeking spending habits. Use of your imagination can often times lead to entertainment without a high price tag, this can help you live a more full life at a greatly reduced cost.

NOTES :

_____

_____

_____

INTELLECTUALIZING YOUR MONEY HABITS

Intellectualize your money habits by taking the emotion out of spending, borrowing, earning, and investing. What does that mean, exactly? Most people who are financially challenged are making financial decisions based on the emotion of the moment in an attempt to try and achieve a certain feeling they desire. By intellectualizing these tasks we can take the emotion out of them. Our monetary actions must fall in line with our well thought out wealth building plan, not our short-term desires for a particular feeling.

I'm not saying we should become mathematical robots... After all, emotions are what truly living is all about. I just want you to implement a strategy that will help keep your finances off the emotional roller coaster ride. Although some people make big, obvious mistakes that set them back financially, most people have a far more subtle method of destroying their fiscal future.

If it's small things that cause us big trouble, shouldn't that make it easier to fix? That may sound all and well but isn't necessarily the case. You will work hard to avoid big losses, but if you do happen upon one you will surely feel the pain and remember it for a long time. This natural form of punishment can make it far easier to maintain your focus and avoid a repeat. The wealth building game can be easily won or lost due to small decisions, especially for people with limited incomes. So to win the money game, we need to focus on the small underestimated aspects. When you look at the value of a dollar, for example, you can see how little things can add up to huge financial differences.

While some people will hesitate to spend $100, they can more easily justify multiple small purchases. These simple justifications can often add up to well over the $100 they were trying to avoid spending in the first place. Have you ever looked at your bank statement and thought, "Where'd the money go?" You look over the entire list and not one purchase was over $100, yet somehow $500 or even $1,000 is gone. If you look closer you're bound to see the many infamous $17 coffee shop charges that you made to comfort yourself about not making that big purchase. Now your good feelings are gone and the negative despair has set in because you are once again broke. In the end, you got a few momentary pleasures while you were financially stepping backwards.

That was feel-good emotional spending—not an intellectualized financial decision. An intellectualized financial strategy will include provisions for your emotional satisfaction but in a way that is in balance with your overall financial goals. That's all we want: just balance. You *can* achieve a great life and emotional balance by making habits that don't set you back financially.

We all have moments of emotional weakness. They come in many forms and work to destroy us financially, and yet they are typically small and pervasive. We are often inclined to make foolish money moves out of guilt, our desire to feel good, or in an attempt to help others. Sometimes an effort to make financial progress even makes us vulnerable to deals that are actually too good to be true.

Take, for example, a member of your family that often comes to you to borrow money and that you know is always broke. You don't need to loan them money, and you probably shouldn't. Loaning money to someone you know is not likely to pay you back can make you just as financially "wise" as they are. The end result is you both will likely end up broke.

I know this can be hard with family, but we need to look at our money decisions intellectually. If you come from a poor family or have poor friends, the last thing you want to do is take financial advice from them, loan them money, or live your life in a similar fashion. Many people end up unintentionally adopting the bad behavior of those with whom they surround themselves with, eventually picking up poor financial habits by some crazy form of osmosis.

If osmosis is going to dominate the game, then I want to hang around people that know how to handle money and pick up *their* habits, not the other way around. When you think, "Should I loan money to this person that is broke and obviously has poor financial habits?" Thoroughly think that decision through. You will find that 99% of the time the answer is no.

If you are not (and have not previously been) wealthy, the odds are already stacked against you. It will become an impossible battle if you start taking on and covering the costs of those around you. Without a doubt, looseness of that kind will lead to your financial doom.

If you don't have money, you likely understand better than most the pain of not having it. Consequently, you may be very inclined to attempt to help others out when they are struggling. This is a noble cause, and giving is very rewarding (I greatly encourage it), but splitting your last dollar is not going to help anyone out. It will just create two losers. The best way to help someone who is financially struggling is not to give them money, but rather to be a good role model. Share what you learn here and show them the way to financial prosperity. Show them how they can intellectualize their financial habits and not give in to moments of emotional weakness.

People will often look at the rich and think they are greedy because they partake in so much while others hurt financially. However, anyone that understands money knows that giving to people with bad money habits will only lead to *everyone* being broke. On average, rich people give far more to good causes than people who aren't (and I'm not talking about the total dollar amount, but rather as a percentage of their wealth). They typically do it in a way that provides opportunities for people to improve their own lives, not to just improve it *for* them. Giving in a way that helps lead someone to improving their own situation provides dignity to the receiver and creates an environment with more opportunities for everyone.

There's an old Chinese proverb that says: **"Give a man a fish and he will eat for a day; teach a man to fish and he will eat for a lifetime."**

What I hope you will take from this is that everyone needs to know how to fish, so to speak. One of the best ways to learn is by teaching, so convey this information to those around you who might need to learn some of your proverbial fishing skills. Only a fool would give a fish to someone who is unwilling to learn to fish for themselves.

Living a poor life because you gave everything you have away, regardless of the good intention, does not make you a better person— only a poor one. By being financially successful and leading by example you will be able to afford to do far more good that will last.

ASSET ALLOCATIONS SIMPLIFIED

Improper asset allocation can unnecessarily leave the door open for wealth destruction. It can possibly even bring devastation to someone who appears very financially successful. The Wealth Builder program guidelines give you broad directions as to how you want to allocate your assets, but you need to think your allocations through even further.

Although there are some exceptions to the rule, a very diverse asset allocation approach will be best for most people. A professional investor may tie up a disproportionately large portion of their wealth in one asset class that they are an expert in, but such an approach rapidly increases the risk of a large loss (especially for the non-expert). The average person should not dump a substantial amount of their wealth into any one asset class, regardless of how great the opportunity. If anyone tells you different, they are of the get-rich-quick mentality and I would seek your financial advice from another source.

The following are some general principles for allocating your assets.

NOTES :

_____

_____

_____

_____

_____

_____

Security Cushion

Your security cushion should be divided into different assets to protect its value. I advise you to divide your security cushion into three eventually equal categories, funding the first category fully, then the second, and lastly the third.

1. **Cash** - Cash should be stored in an interest-bearing savings account.
2. **Investments** – Liquid money market or low-risk mutual funds should be utilized.
3. **Precious Metals** – Personally, I like owning physical gold and silver as opposed to electronically traded funds (ETFs). The primary drawback of owning precious metals physically is the buying and selling transaction costs. That being said, you are looking to hold on to this long term for a rainy day so it shouldn't be an issue. I said to invest in the other two categories first because this will be the last asset accessed should you need it.

Security Investments

Security investments should be all low-risk, including your home. Although some may not think of a home as a good investment anymore, you do need a place to live and if you have a mortgage then any additional investment you make into your home earns a return simply by saving you interest.

My personal favorite security investments are low-risk growth mutual funds (with a good track record of at least five years), Certificates of Deposit (CDs), and government-issued securities (savings bonds, treasury bonds, notes, and bills). The last two can be good options, but there are a couple of things to keep in mind: CDs don't usually outperform inflation adequately, and although government securities can appear safe, they can also be volatile. Also, government securities don't typically keep pace with the returns offered by mutual fund equities, but remember—this section is just about diversity to protect against individual assets taking hits.

Keep these three things in mind: diversity, liquidity, and inflation. You don't want to dump all your money into your home because that would be neither liquid nor diverse. Spread your investments around. If you only have a limited amount to invest, begin by investing in only one or two classes for four to six months and then alternate. Make sure your investments will outpace the rate of inflation, preferably by 3% or greater. I use 4% as my base rate of inflation (which may be high or low on some years but on average is probably a safe estimate).

Growth Investments

I think a diversified basket full of mutual funds from multiple categories is the best vehicle for this type of investment. Specifically, these three different kinds:

- Growth and income - ⅓
- Aggressive growth - ⅓
- International fund - ⅓

There are other investment allocation strategies out there, but I like this one because it is simple and fairly safe. As you approach retirement, consider cutting your aggressive growth holdings. When you are ten years from retirement, reduce your risky contributions by 20% each year. For your last five working years, reallocate 20% per year of the remaining aggressive growth balance in to safer funds.

Business Investments

The primary goal here is either to get higher returns than mutual funds can provide or obtain better asset diversification. One vehicle for this entails investing directly into businesses (in the event that a good, relatively secure opportunity comes up). Another includes investing in real estate for the long hold or buying fixer-uppers to resell. Depending on your financial status, you may be able to buy established businesses that can be managed by others such as a bar, resort, recreational vehicle park, or other turnkey business.

Remember, it takes business savvy to own a business regardless of whether it will be managed by others or not. Business investments are not for everyone. You should not do something that you are uncomfortable with or that will put you at unnecessary risk. If the business class of investments is not right for you, just put your allocations into your more aggressive growth mutual funds.

NOTES :

_____

_____

_____

_____

_____

_____

_____

_____

_____

_____

_____

_____

_____

MONEY-WISE AUTO-BUYING GUIDE

This is one of my favorite tools for making big swings in people's abilities to build and protect their wealth. Cars have always been a terrible investment due to their depreciating nature, but there are things you can do to help minimize their wealth destruction. There are many different ways to evaluate car purchases, but here is the Wealth Builder Lifestyle's method.

Initial Depreciation

We all want and love new cars. They come with the pride of being the first owner of a vehicle, that great new car smell (which is created by the chemical off-gassing of the car's components, by the way), and the excitement of driving it home for the first time. This is an emotional motivation that has a high cost. Until you are so well off that you just have money to burn, take this into consideration: you can expect the value of your new vehicle to drop by approximately 10% the minute you drive it off the lot and another 10% by the time you get a few miles on it. Plus there's the tax and licensing, which will run you about another 10%. So to experience the thrill of buying a $30,000 car new, could cost you $6,600 in the first few months of ownership. You had better really love that new car smell, because you paid a small fortune for it.

Fastest Depreciation

The first 36,000 miles (usually two to three years of age) has the second highest depreciation cost. You can expect this to create a loss of value of another 15-20% of the total value of your purchase. When thinking about depreciation, take into consideration that the second 36,000 miles will depreciate your value by only about half as much as the first

267

(and similarly the third only half as much as the second). Therefore, the actual cash lost to depreciation for time and mileage is less and less as the vehicle gets older. You will always have depreciation costs no matter what automobile it is, but over time they may become negligible.

Many people buy new because they don't want to have to worry about breakdowns or repairs. This is a legitimate concern, but with the quality of cars built today the likelihood of a breakdown or major repair between 36,000 and 100,000 miles is actually very low. The Wealth Builder Lifestyle recommendation for people that want to drive new cars is to buy them when they are *virtually* new, so a few years old when the vehicle has around 36,000 miles on it. By this point, someone else has already taken the financial hit of the two largest depreciation periods. Not only will this save you from wealth lost to massive depreciation, but it will also save you from higher taxes, licensing fees, and loan interest (since your values will all be based on a reduced sale price).

Cost of Ownership

Another aspect of car purchasing to be aware of is the cost of ownership, the biggest of which is usually fuel. We all want a vehicle that gets good gas mileage, but how important of a consideration is this for you? If fuel costs $3.25 a gallon and you drive 12,000 miles per year (which is an average value), a vehicle that gets 20 miles per gallon (MPG) will cost you $54 per month more to own than one that gets 30 MPG. Most people don't sweat the small dollars, so if you don't typically pay much heed to the MPG of a car you're not alone. Consider this: if you got the 30 MPG car and put the money you saved to work wealth builder style starting at the age of 18, then by the time you are 65, that little $54 monthly difference (a $30,500 total investment over the example period) could be worth $698,000 (based on a modest and achievable 10% return on investment).

Larger vehicles that get less miles per gallon will also usually cost more to maintain due to a larger oil capacity, bigger tires, and so on. I'm not saying bigger or smaller is better. They both have their pros and cons and for some situations there is no substitute for a superior vehicle.

One of the major goals I had for this program was to get people to start evaluating purchases with the lifetime cost in mind. My hope is that maybe then we will all have more appreciation for the true value of our money and financial decisions. Although $54 a month today doesn't seem like a big deal, it could get you over half way to retiring a millionaire. Use the following forms to help evaluate different car purchases. This can be an enlightening experience and if nothing else will help make you a more informed buyer.

We are going to evaluate your purchase in four areas:

- **Total purchase cost** – the total amount of cash you will actually spend to buy the car

- **Five-year depreciation** – the amount of the total purchase cost that the vehicle will lose in value over the next five years

- **Total monthly cost** – the estimated monthly cost for each option, including fuel, maintenance/repairs, and payments (adjusted by individual vehicle type)

- **Wealth impact** – how this will affect your long-term wealth picture (can vary greatly by vehicle)

NOTES :

_____

_____

_____

_____

Use this form to determine the total overall purchase cost of a vehicle. If you are paying cash for the vehicle, just enter the total vehicle cost (including tax and license fees) in the Total Purchase Cost box. For an accurate comparison, any financed vehicles should be amortized over five years (although when you make your actual purchase I would obviously advise you to get as short of a loan as possible.)

Auto Purchase Analyzer			
Cost	Option One	Option Two	Option Three
Monthly Payment	$_____	$_____	$_____
Loan Length (in months)	× _____	× _____	× _____
Total of Payments (payment × months)	= $_____	= $_____	= $_____
Down Payment (plus any other cash expenses)	+ $_____	+ $_____	+ $_____
Total Purchase Cost (down payment + total of payments)	= $_____	= $_____	= $_____

NOTES :

_____

_____

_____

_____

_____

_____

MONEY-WISE AUTO-BUYING GUIDE

Use the Total Purchase Cost from the previous form in the following one. The depreciation (as it's known to most people) is evaluated by subtracting the End Value from the Purchase Price. A more realistic approach is to base it on the total amount of value left after all your purchase costs (which includes your financing cost). The difference between that and the End Value is the true loss you sustained on this vehicle over five years. Of course, no dealer or bank wants to point this out to you. Very few ever even consider it (much less calculate it), which is why so many have no idea how much wealth they are potentially wasting on vehicles.

Auto Comparison Overview				
Five-Year Depreciation Cost				
Rate Modifier Descriptions	ACMT average car or mini truck	LS luxury or sports car	S4X SUV or 4x4 truck	FS full size pickup or van
Brand New	ACMT = 0.45	LS = 0.35	S4X = 0.45	FS = 0.4
Used	ACMT = 0.5	LS = 0.3	S4X = 0.35	FS = 0.5

Option One

Total Purchase Cost = $_____

Purchase Price   Rate Modifier   End Value

_____ $_____   ×   _____   = $_____

Total Wealth Lost (Total Purchase Cost – End Value) = $_____

Option Two

Total Purchase Cost = $_____

Purchase Price   Rate Modifier   End Value

_____ $_____   ×   _____   = $_____

Total Wealth Lost (Total Purchase Cost – End Value) = $_____

Option Three

Total Purchase Cost = $_____

Purchase Price   Rate Modifier   End Value

_____ $_____   ×   _____   = $_____

Total Wealth Lost (Total Purchase Cost – End Value) = $_____

The following form will help you get a better idea of the true monthly cost of purchasing and owning the different types of vehicles you are considering. There are a couple of key factors to consider regarding costs outside of the purchase price. Typically the larger and fancier the car the more it costs to operate and maintain.

NOTES :

_____

_____

_____

_____

_____

_____

_____

_____

_____

_____

_____

_____

_____

_____

_____

_____

MONEY-WISE AUTO-BUYING GUIDE

Detailed Auto Comparison		
Annual Miles	**Monthly Miles** (annual ÷ 12)	**Total Miles** (annual × 5)
_____	_____	_____

Maintenance by Vehicle Type	**ACMT** = Compact or mid-sized car, compact truck **LST** = Luxury or sports car, SUV, 4×4, full size truck	
Less than 60,000 miles	ACMT = $0.04	LST = $0.07
60,000 to 120,000 miles	ACMT = $0.06	LST = $0.10
More than 120,000 miles	ACMT = $0.10	LST = $0.15

Option One

Fuel Cost per Gallon
$_____ ÷ MPG _____ = Cost per Mile $_____

Maintenance by Vehicle Type (from chart above)	$_____
Fuel Cost per Mile + Maintenance by Vehicle Type	$_____
Monthly Miles (from above)	_____
(Fuel + Maintenance) × Monthly Miles	$_____
Monthly Payment	$_____

Total Monthly Cost (fuel and maintenance + payment) $_____

Option Two

Fuel Cost per Gallon
$_____ ÷ MPG _____ = Cost per Mile $_____

Maintenance by Vehicle Type (from chart above)	$_____
Fuel Cost per Mile + Maintenance by Vehicle Type	$_____
Monthly Miles (from above)	_____
(Fuel + Maintenance) × Monthly Miles	$_____
Monthly Payment	$_____

Total Monthly Cost (fuel and maintenance + payment) $_____

Option Three

Fuel Cost per Gallon
$_____ ÷ MPG _____ = Cost per Mile $_____

Maintenance by Vehicle Type (from chart above)	$_____
Fuel Cost per Mile + Maintenance by Vehicle Type	$_____
Monthly Miles (from above)	_____
(Fuel + Maintenance) × Monthly Miles	$_____
Monthly Payment	$_____

Total Monthly Cost (Fuel and Maintenance + Payment) $_____

PART THREE: WEALTH BUILDER ESSENTIALS

Last but not least, we want to combine each of the previous variables to determine the overall wealth impact for each potential vehicle. The loss of potential wealth building opportunities is by far the most overlooked and damaging factor in making an auto purchase. The following will calculate the approx. difference based on investing any potential money saved over the five years and then letting it sit in a 10% return investment for 30 years.

Auto Wealth Impact Comparison				
Option One				
Highest Down Payment	**Down Payment** (option one)			**Invested Value**
$_____	- $_____	= $_____	× $28 =	$_____
Highest Monthly Cost	**Monthly Cost** (option one)			**Invested Value**
$_____	- $_____	= $_____	× $1,548 =	$_____
Total End Value (from depreciation form)				$_____
Option One Total (combine all item totals)				$_____
Option Two				
Highest Down Payment	**Down Payment** (option two)			**Invested Value**
$_____	- $_____	= $_____	× $28 =	$_____
Highest Monthly Cost	**Monthly Cost** (option two)			**Invested Value**
$_____	- $_____	= $_____	× $1,548 =	$_____
Total End Value (from depreciation form)				$_____
Option Two Total (combine all item totals)				$_____
Option Three				
Highest Down Payment	**Down Payment** (option three)			**Invested Value**
$_____	- $_____	= $_____	× $28 =	$_____
Highest Monthly Cost	**Monthly Cost** (option three)			**Invested Value**
$_____	- $_____	= $_____	× $1,548 =	$_____
Total End Value (from depreciation form)				$_____
Option Three Total (combine all item totals)				$_____

MONEY-WISE AUTO-BUYING GUIDE

Enter the requested information in the fields below to determine your final comparison results.

Final Auto Comparison					
	Total (from previous)		Total Purchase Cost (page 270)		Total Wealth Impact
Option One	$_____	-	$_____	=	$_____
Option Two	$_____	-	$_____	=	$_____
Option Three	$_____	-	$_____	=	$_____

The higher the wealth impact number the better rated your vehicle is as a wealth builder. Some vehicles may actually come out a negative number (especially if you are only checking one car, since there is no difference that can be invested). I hope this has successfully illustrated the value of buying less than you can afford and investing the difference.

NOTES :

_____

_____

_____

_____

_____

_____

_____

_____

_____

_____

LUXURY PURCHASE ANALYSIS TOOL

We've talked about the adverse affects spending can have on wealth building primarily in regards to small purchases. Now we are going to talk about the real fun—big purchases like boats, RVs, and those other luxury items we buy when we start to get ahead financially.

It's a little ironic to me that when we finally start getting ahead, that's when we are most likely to make a huge purchasing mistake. Unfortunately, that one stroke of a pen can destroy large amounts of our net worth instantly. I'm not trying to be overly dramatic here—every year millions of people in the US make foolish large purchases that result in substantial losses in net worth. It's about more than just setting you back on cash for a down payment (which, done wisely, doesn't necessarily hurt your net worth so much as reallocate it to a different asset).

There are six key points of consideration for wealth builders when it comes to making any large purchase.

Can you really afford it?

I'm not talking about whether or not you can come up with the down payment or meet the monthly costs. You need to ensure that when you purchase this you will still be able to make all of your saving and investment contributions in full as planned. If not, you can't afford it and a true wealth builder wouldn't buy it.

What will it cost to own?

Things like boats and RVs may require additional costs. You may need to insure it, pay taxes on it, store it, maintain it, and so on. All of those items are wealth eaters, so you need to be sure you can also afford to throw that money away.

What is the initial depreciation?

This is the total loss you will take the moment you sign the paperwork. If you are buying a new RV, for instance, the day you drive it off the lot it will likely lose about 20% in value, which comes directly off your net worth. So if you have $200,000 in net worth and go buy a $150,000 RV, the day you drive it off the lot it will depreciate $30,000 (plus whatever your initial tax, license, and other fees are) which will cause your net worth to instantly drop to less than $170,000. If you add that RV to your balance sheet at the purchase price, shame on you. You're only fooling yourself.

What is the future depreciation?

Most material possessions (outside of houses) are depreciating assets. Some are even quickly depreciating assets. A wealth builder will evaluate how long they plan to hold on to that RV, for example, and what they will be able to recover when they sell it. In the case of that $150,000 RV, I would estimate that after 15 years its market value (what you could actually sell it for) would be about $22,500, or 15% of what you paid for it. So your future depreciation would be another $97,500. Keep in mind, this doesn't include the interest you paid on the loan (if you financed it), storage, insurance, maintenance, or repair costs over those 15 years.

What is the total purchase cost?

Using the price of the item is not typically representative of the real cost because it doesn't include your finance charges. On the other hand, if you paid cash, great! You don't need to worry about this.

What will this cost you in lost investment wealth?

This is probably one of the least looked at and most important considerations for a wealth builder. Being a wealth builder means you are continually growing your wealth. This means you not only have to

278

offset any cost you spend, but you also have to look at the impact it has on your ability to generate wealth.

I'm going to show you a simple way to evaluate and make better buying decisions. Notice I didn't say "good" or "great" buying decisions, that's because most of these luxury purchases will be nothing of the sort, so we just want to do the best we can. If you are being smart and building wealth you have the right to squander a little bit of it on some extravagances (even if they aren't really great investments).

Use the following form to perform the desired calculations and to determine if you can afford the purchase. If you are buying a used item from a private party, you shouldn't have any initial depreciation. If you buy used from a dealer, use 10% for the initial depreciation factor (which assumes you negotiate and buy well) and 20% if you are buying new. Do a rough guestimate on the repair costs on the item during your time of ownership, divide that by the months owned, and include it in the Other category under Monthly Ownership Expenses.

NOTES :

_____

_____

_____

_____

_____

_____

_____

_____

Luxury Purchase Depreciation Evaluator

Purchase Price	One-Time Fees	Total Purchase Cost
(excluding taxes and fees)	(taxes, setup, deliver, etc.)	(total initial purchase cost)
$ _____	+ $ _____	= $ _____

Down Payment	Monthly Ownership Expenses	Combine the Monthly Ownership Expenses together and enter the monthly total at the bottom. Then, combine the Monthly Payment with the figure you just calculated to find the actual Total Monthly Cost.
$ _____	Insurance $ _____ Tax and Reg. $ _____ Storage $ _____ Other $ _____	

Monthly Payment	Total Monthly Ownership Expenses	Total Monthly Cost
$ _____	+ $ _____	= $ _____

Depreciation

Purchase Price	Depreciation Factor	Initial Depreciation
(excluding tax and fees)	(estimated initial depreciation percentage)	
$ _____	× 0.00 (0%, for private party) 0.10 (10%, for dealer used) 0.20 (20%, for new)	= $ _____

Purchase Price - Initial Depreciation =	Blue Book Value at Resale (likely resale value)	+ Total Depreciation During Use
$ _____	- $ _____	= $ _____
		=

Total Lifetime Depreciation	$ _____

NOTES :

_____

_____

LUXURY PURCHASE ANALYSIS TOOL

To calculate the total impact the purchase will have on your wealth over the time span of ownership, complete the next form. It will require the use of amortization and compound interest calculators which can easily be found online, or at the following links:

- http://www.interestcalc.org

- http://www.amortization-calc.com

Don't short yourself by skipping this exercise as it's great knowledge for understanding how to evaluate a purchase of any kind. Once you understand this concept you can apply it to almost anything you buy to make better decisions. The person selling you something isn't going to help you look at the purchase this way, so learn how to do it yourself.

Luxury Purchase Wealth Impact Evaluator			
Amortization Calculation		**Compound Interest Calculation**	
Total Financed (loan amount)	$_____	Down Payment (initial investment)	$_____
Loan Length (in years)	_____	Interest Rate	10%
Interest Rate	____%	Regular Investment (enter monthly ownership expenses)	$_____
Total Principle and Interest Payment	$_____	Loan Length (in years)	_____
Total Loan Cost	$_____	Total Investment Value	$_____
Combined Total (negative wealth impact)		$_____	

The wealth impact is a little skewed because this amount is how much you would have by not making the purchase. If you actually did complete the transaction, you would still have a residual value equal to what that item could be sold for. You can run one more calculation for a more precise wealth impact evaluation by simply deducting the asset resale value from the total negative wealth impact. Just keep in mind that you also have the cost of use, which includes things like fuel or other related expenses that would be incurred while using the item. This is money that you would not be spending if you didn't make the purchase, so ultimately those would go against the asset resale value too.

      Were you surprised at what the real cost of your purchase was? We are trained to always focus on the sticker price. Few (if any) people you asked could actually tell you what the real cost of making a purchase is. Now you will have the edge and can not only answer that question but also help educate friends and family so they too can make better purchasing decisions.

NOTES :

_____

_____

_____

_____

_____

_____

_____

_____

_____

_____

_____

_____

_____

_____

"BEAT THE BANK" HOMEOWNERSHIP

"Homeownership" and "bank" don't belong in the same sentence. The whole premise of owning your home is that you own it (and are therefore free of the bank). To be clear, I'm not against banks or financing as there are few that would ever have the discipline to save up enough money to buy a home outright. Where people usually go wrong in buying their home is in how they finance and pay off their loans. Here are some sample results for a $150,000 home that can be achieved with the method I'm going to share with you.

Typical Method

Time to Pay Off: **30 Years**

Sample Mortgage Amount: **$150,000**

Monthly Payment Based on 30 years at 5% APR: **$805.23**

Total Loan Interest Paid: **$139,884**

Total Cost to Pay off Loan: **$289,884**

Wealth Builder Method

Time to Pay Off: **15 Years**

Sample Mortgage Amount: **$150,000**

Accelerated Beginning Payment at 5% APR: **$986.21**

Accelerated Ending Payment at 5% APR: **$1,607.12**

Total Loan Interest Paid: **$70,098**

Total Cost to Pay off Loan: **$220,098**

Net Difference

1. Paid off 15 years sooner
2. $70,000 Less Interest Paid

Here is the Wealth Builder strategy for financing and paying off your home that will help you avoid the home buyer pitfalls that the banks prosper on. Work through the process of finding out exactly what the numbers would be on your home or on a home you may be considering buying.

Ideally we would all get 10- or 15-year loans and pay our homes off expeditiously to avoid paying ridiculous amounts of interest. Unfortunately, with the loose credit markets and an endless supply of fools lining up to buy homes they can't afford, home prices have been artificially elevated. This greatly limits the ability for most to afford to finance and pay off our homes with short-term mortgages.

Here is a simple strategy that any homebuyer should be able to use and afford. This will allow you to greatly reduce the interest paid over the life of the loan and pay your home off in half the time. If you can't afford to use this strategy, you are probably not in a position to afford a house.

First, finance your home with a 30-year **fixed rate mortgage with no prepayment penalties**. The last part is very important. Some banks get you in to a loan and want to keep you there, reaping large profits as long as they can. Should you decide to pay your loan off early they will aim to nail you with ridiculous costs to secure they still get their profits. You may already be in a loan with prepayment penalties, and if that is the case so be it. It still probably makes sense to just eat the cost of the penalties and get it paid off. Often times you can get around these penalties by refinancing and fully paying off the loan as then the penalties typically are not applicable.

Our goal is to cut your loan repayment time in half without putting you on the edge financially (which is why I don't advise locking yourself in to a shorter term loan initially). Next, collect the following information about your loan:

"BEAT THE BANK" HOME OWNERSHIP

Current Loan Balance: $_____

Length left on loan: Years_____ Months_____

Your Loan Interest Rate: _____%

Current Payment: $_____

Then, you need to get an amortization schedule based on your loan terms; you can use an online calculator to create it (such as the one at http://www.amortization-calc.com). Enter values to the closest tenth of a year (for example if you have 26 and ½ years left enter it as 26.5). Then select "Amortization: show by month" and press Calculate. Printing this schedule out or saving it as a PDF would be helpful for future reference.

So here's how this method works: you are going to pay your regular monthly payment plus the principal portion of the following month's payment. For month one you will end up paying the full amount for the first month plus the principal of the 2nd, on month two you will pay your regular payment amount (which is what shows up for the 3rd month on your amortization schedule) plus the principal amount of the 4th month. An easy way to do this is to print out the amortization schedule and (starting with month two) highlight every other month. Each time you make a payment, work down the list of highlighted months and add that principal amount to your normal payment.

Note: You should check with your lender to see what specifically you need to do if anything to make a principle reduction payment. They may automatically apply the over-payment towards your principal balance, or they may (for example) want you to write a separate check with "pay towards principal" in the memo line.

Fill in your info to come up with the next twelve months of payments. Use the principal amount from your amortization schedule for the month advised in this form.

Accelerated Mortgage Payment Schedule			
Monthly Principal	Normal Payment	Additional Principal	Total Payment
1 _____	$_____	+ (month 2) $_____ =	$_____
2 _____	$_____	+ (month 4) $_____ =	$_____
3 _____	$_____	+ (month 6) $_____ =	$_____
4 _____	$_____	+ (month 8) $_____ =	$_____
5 _____	$_____	+ (month 10) $_____ =	$_____
6 _____	$_____	+ (month 12) $_____ =	$_____
7 _____	$_____	+ (month 14) $_____ =	$_____
8 _____	$_____	+ (month 16) $_____ =	$_____
9 _____	$_____	+ (month 18) $_____ =	$_____
10 _____	$_____	+ (month 20) $_____ =	$_____
11 _____	$_____	+ (month 22) $_____ =	$_____
12 _____	$_____	+ (month 24) $_____ =	$_____

Now, here is some great news: if you follow the payment schedule above for the next twelve months you will have shortened your loan by not just one year, but two. Your principal reduction progressively gets larger every month, which is why your payment changes. If you want to keep things simple, take the total payment from month 6 and pay that amount all year long. The results will be virtually identical, but keep in mind you will still need to recalculate your payment amount every year to keep up.

So, let's look at the fruits of your labor. Aside from paying your home off much sooner (which you won't get to enjoy until later), let's look at your realized wealth creation.

"BEAT THE BANK" HOME OWNERSHIP

Combine the Additional Principal payment amounts you made over the one-year period and enter the amount below:

Additional One-Year Principal Reduction: $_____

This is the additional amount of your home that you now own. No-brainer, right? You paid that amount—it makes sense. Now let's look at the amount of wealth you protected. By being disciplined and taking this little extra step each month, you are greatly reducing the amount of money you will have to pay to get your home's deed in hand.

Look at your amortization chart and run the following calculation. Use the combined amount of your principal and interest payment (*not* the actual amount of your payment, which includes unavoidable taxes and insurance).

Accelerated Mortgage (One-Year, Wealth Saved)
Principal and Interest Payment × 12 = $_____
-
Total Additional Principal Paid $_____
=
Total Wealth Saved $_____

The Total Wealth Saved plus your Total Additional Principal Paid is all the wealth that you have protected using this method. Not only have you secured a larger portion of your house (via additional principal payments), but you've also avoided roughly a year's worth of interest payments ($7,450 or more in squandered wealth based on our $150,000 example home). So essentially your extra $184 monthly payment has saved you an additional $621 per month. That's not a bad return on investment.

The reason I promote this strategy is because (just like getting a 15-year mortgage) your home is paid off sooner, which saves you huge amounts of interest and makes you a true homeowner in half the time.

It also allows flexibility in your monthly overhead should you have an emergency and have to skip paying the increased amount for a month or two (which results in additional financial security). If you're locked in to a higher loan payment from a 15-year mortgage and your income gets disrupted, your home could be put at risk.

Also, with the wealth builder approach your payment starts low and consistently increases over time until you are eventually paying approximately twice as much. You may wonder, "How in the heck will I ever be able to afford that?" Herein lies the beauty of this method: your income will be growing and going up over time as your payment increases, so it won't necessarily be any more of a burden.

Let's look at the big picture to see the dramatic difference you can expect to achieve using this method. Go back to the amortization tool you are using. Enter your loan information and calculate the total principal and interest to pay off your loan as it stands today. If this is a new home you are considering purchasing, use the 30-year term for your loan length parameter. Then perform the same calculation based on paying your loan off in 15 years and enter both the numbers below.

Accelerated Mortgage Wealth Saved	
Total Paid for Current Loan (after 30 years):	$ _____
	-
Total Paid for Accelerated Payoff (after 15 years):	$ _____
	=
Total Wealth Saved:	$ _____

That's a large sum of money saved that otherwise would have been profit for a bank!

NOTES :

_____

_____

"BEAT THE BANK" HOME OWNERSHIP
Fifteen Years Later

Now that you own your home outright, what are you going to do with the remaining 15 years that you would've been making payments? How about investing the money you would've been paying towards your mortgage every month for the next 15 years? While your slow-paying pal is still trying to earn ownership of his home, you'll be scot-free to invest and earn revenue on that freed up money from no longer having a house payment. The picture would look like this (based on our $150,000 example, with an investment annual return of 10%):

Monthly Investment Amount: **$805.23**

Months to Contribute: **180**

Total Contributed to Investment: **$145,000**

Total Investment Value: **$337,000**

Add in the value of the example home (which would have a value of approximately $272,000 based on a 2% annual appreciation over the 30-year period). Your total wealth amassed via this prospect alone would be close to $609,000.

This approach differs from the advice many financial experts give, which is based on creating the maximum amount of wealth in the shortest period of time. Typically, advisors would advocate for investing the extra mortgage money at a 10% interest return, essentially leveraging the bank's money. The reasoning is, if you are only paying 5% interest on the bank's money, why rush to pay that off when you can get a 10% return by investing?

The reason the former method is superior is because both investing and carrying a mortgage are gambling. I want to minimize risk and keep my exposure low in case things go bad, especially since history proves they can and will. If you invested that principal overpayment instead over the first 15 years and then let it sit for the next 15 (continuing to pay off the example loan in 30 years) then at a

10% interest rate your total wealth created from investing would be about $614,000. Add in the value of the $272,000 home and you have created $886,000, or $277,000 more than the wealth builder scenario. The math on that one's a bit crazy and the increase is tempting but ultimately not worth the extra risk, and I'm going to explain why.

What happens if 15 years into your aggressive investment plan you only have your home half paid for and the economy takes a dive? The stock market could get cut in half like it did in 2009. That rosy picture could end up looking like this: your investment account after 15 years amassed a value of $147,000, but due to the recession it is cut in half down to $73,500. Your home value (which has appreciated to $202,000) took a 30% hit because of the poor economy, and now has a value of $141,000. What's more is you still owe $115,000 on it! Your 15-year net value (based on the investments and your house) would total about $100,000. Doesn't seem too bad, right? On the other hand, if you had chosen to pay off your home you would be worth at least $41,000 more (thanks to having your $141,000 home paid for). This just shows one situation where if you had invested instead of paying off your home you would actually be in a far worse financial situation.

If for some reason you lost your job and you had to cash in your investments, you would likely have to pay taxes and possibly even penalties on that money. It would dramatically shrink the value of your investments and force you to use that money to cover house payments so you don't lose it to foreclosure. The result is that most of what you would pay is eaten by interest, destroying even more wealth. If you end up burning through all your money, you could end up putting your home equity and personal security at risk. The outcome could be disastrous, leaving you with bad credit and forcing you in to the rental market.

Unfortunately, many people that appeared to have their financial house in order have gone through that exact financial implosion, for no other reason than they were being too aggressive and were blindsided. If you think that sort of thing is a once in a lifetime event and not likely to happen again in your era, think again. Virtually all the circumstances that existed leading up to our last economic freefall are still in place. Worse yet, our national debt and deficit are all out of control. Next time our economy is tested (which I certainly expect I will live to see), we are not going to have the safety net we had in place the last time. Smart, forward-thinking wealth builders are getting prepared to take care of themselves come the worst.

The Wealth Builder Lifestyle is a strategic system that will help keep you as financially strong as possible. Don't get overly greedy. Use the recommended strategy to get your home paid off as soon as you can. Even if you are already halfway done with paying it off, use the accelerated payoff method to shorten your remaining payoff by half.

NOTES :

_____

_____

_____

_____

_____

_____

_____

_____

_____

_____

_____

_____

CONCLUSION

SUCCESSFULLY ACHIEVING GOALS

If you don't currently have specific goals set or you're not taking the actions necessary to reach them, your current habits (good or bad) are determining your goals for you. I'm going to give you four simple questions that if you continually ask yourself, will greatly increase your chances of not only meeting your goals, but exceeding them. It's easy to get caught up in day-to-day activities, get sidetracked from your goals, and lose focus. It happens to all of us. You don't have to stay consciously focused on every aspect of every goal at every moment. If you just focus on these four simple questions, they will keep you from getting off track. You can use this little acronym to help you remember them.

P.E.T.S (Plan, Effective, Tool, Status)

(P – Plan) Does this support my plan?

Any time you step outside the daily habits that are aligned with your overall goals, ask yourself, "Does this support my plan? Will taking this action move me closer to or further away from my goal?" This is applicable to any variation in your life. Ask it when you're deciding whether to go out to dinner, a movie, or on a vacation. Even when you're assessing small deviations like purchasing a biscotti with your coffee, be conscious of this question. Each action we take has a positive or negative effect on our life, so asking this question will help ensure you stay focused on the positives and avoid the negatives.

(E – Effective) Is this the most effective way?

When you do make a change outside your normal routine, perhaps you will find it's positive and for the best. However, take your consideration one step further. Ask, "Is this the most effective way to get the results I desire?" Consider all your options. If it's not, take the more effective alternative you come up with. We want momentum. We don't just want to do the bare minimum and get good results, we want to get the *best* results. When you consistently get great results, not only are you going to achieve your goals much faster but you're also going to become a stronger, more successful person overall.

(T – Tool) Is there a tool that can help?

Often we think that what we know or currently think about is all there is. Break out of that mindset. Look outside your usual environment for tools that can help you get better results and make more informed decisions. This will help you excel beyond your current abilities. When it comes to wealth building, you need to actually **use** the tools in this program. Do not just read through them once. If you're going to buy a car or a luxury item, for example, use the tools within to refresh your thoughts and make sure you continually make the best decisions.

Thinking about a job change? Go back through the career section of this book and make sure you aren't slipping into an old, limiting pattern. It may simply help you remember why you are where you are and realize that right now a change just isn't right for you. Always keep sharpening your tools and looking for the best ways to get results.

(S – Status) What is my status?

Ask yourself, "What is my status?" It's great to stay focused and effectively moving forward, but part of staying motivated is recognizing your growth. How much progress have you made? How much closer to your goal are you? Connect your focus and actions with your results so you can clearly see the benefits of your efforts and sacrifices. There is amazing power in measuring your results and knowing where you are, how fast you're making advancements, and when you will achieve your goal. Don't leave yourself guessing: get clarity and stay driven.

Rewarding Results

Remember to use that fun money and reward yourself for good results. Part of sticking with any plan is rewarding yourself when you do stick with it. Don't underestimate the power of dangling a metaphorical carrot in front of yourself as motivation. If you have been diligent and successful in living the Wealth Builder Lifestyle, don't be afraid to make some temporary (but safe and well thought out) exceptions to the rules for a greater reward. Not only is doing so okay, but I actually *encourage* you to do this each time you achieve a substantial benchmark. Don't do it randomly—make the most of these larger rewards by setting your benchmarks and rewards in advance. Keep your plunder in proportion to your achievement. Say, for instance, you successfully pay off $10,000 in debt. Maybe after that you could set aside your debt reduction contributions until you save up $500 to take a weekend trip to some place you really love. Decide on your benchmarks and rewards early on, and then start planning immediately so that each positive step towards it is associated with being one step closer to whatever your reward is.

Have some fun with it. You can be focusing on multiple goals and rewards at the same time. Let's say that in five years when the house is paid off you're going to take a cruise to the Bahamas for your reward—no problem! Get some literature from your travel agent or the cruise line about the specific cruise you want to take. Start looking into and planning your trip with the expectation that you will achieve your goal on or before the target date so you can be on that cruise. Use something you really want that will motivate you and that you will really appreciate after all the hard work.

GRATITUDE AND CONTRIBUTION

When it comes to being truly wealthy, gratitude and contribution are powerful players. As you begin achieving your personal dreams, don't forget all the people and opportunities that made it all possible. Sure, you are the one working your butt off—and that is admirable—but nothing happens on behalf of oneself exclusively. Having an attitude of gratitude along with your material wealth will not only make you the admiration of others, but it will also fill you up on the inside, something money alone will never be able to do.

Pay it forward: contribute back to your community by sharing your wisdom and putting a percentage of your financial means into achieving something good. I think we all know about the unique needs of those around us, so it's less about the vehicle we choose to use and more about the impact. If we all donated our time and money to the same causes, many other great causes would end up neglected, slipping through the cracks and not getting the attention they need.

I personally think that if we all contributed a combination of our time, energy, and/or financial resources toward solving a problem or helping to fulfill a need that we are uniquely aware of, we could dramatically change the world for the better. It's easy for those who figure out the system of life to receive wealth in abundance, but if we don't give back we will be living a self-serving and unfulfilling life of greed. Not contributing defies the inherent values of humanity, which will internally take its toll and never allow complete fulfillment to those of us who skimp on giving back.

For example, I will donate a substantial number of copies of this book to less fortunate individuals and organizations that help people suffering from financial hardships. This is a unique opportunity that I have to give back and contribute through my work. You need to look for the chances *you* have—they're all around you.

MONEY MENTOR FOR KIDS

As parents, we all have a moral obligation to pass on good wealth building skills to our children. But how? Most parents I talk to are focused on learning to master wealth themselves, leaving their kids to pick up their own habits through watching others or through personal life experiences. Leaving them to fend for themselves may have merit, but leaving it up to chance is not a good way to set up our children for success.

I have included a simple wealth-mastery plan for parents to use with their children. This plan can be adapted to be utilized with very young children but in my opinion should be a must for children 10 years or older.

We severely underestimate our children's learning abilities, especially when it comes to money. We have christened money as "adult talk," therefore failing to proactively make efforts to help our kids understand money at higher levels. What's more is we've often gone out of our way to keep them from seeing our relevant struggles and successes. We think we are doing them a favor by not burdening them with concerns about money management. I'm not saying we should burden our children with our financial problems. But we want them to understand and appreciate how money works in the real world so they are prepared to succeed financially. Kids were born to learn—let them learn! A hard time can be one of the most beneficial learning experiences a child can have.

One day it occurred to me that I was studying the lessons I should have already known about money, yet doing nothing to ensure my kids didn't follow in my footsteps. So I initially created this plan to help me educate my kids financially. It worked, so I want to share it with you.

CONCLUSION
Program Outline

I hope that if you have kids this simple program can work as well for yours as it did for mine. On the next page is a Paycheck Calculator (timecard), this is used to track their daily performance. You may be thinking, "I've seen these," or, "I've tried something like this and it never works." I've been there and done that as well, but this is different. Each chore has a daily monetary value. You will decide each chore and how much each is worth. Yes, you will be paying your kids to perform—it's a lot like the real world, so they better get used to it!

Here is the deal: you are going to be turning over financial responsibility to them for some key expenses, such as things they want and are motivated to get. Their pay should not be akin to the small allowance most people give their children. Rather, this should be a decent sum of money. You will be turning over financial control for things like their personal expenses, fun money, and even some investment funds.

In the following worksheet, divide the total pay you will be putting on the table each week by seven and enter that amount for the Total Daily Pay. Then divide that amount by the total Number of Jobs you will have for them to do (which will determine the daily pay rate per job).

Per Job Pay Rate (Money Mentor)			
Total Weekly Pay	Total Daily Pay	Number of Jobs	Pay Rate Per Job
$_____ ÷ 7 =	$_____	÷ _____ =	$_____

You'll also want to choose jobs that will help them establish good lifelong habits. Think of what skills you want your children to make habitual that will have lasting value. The habits that allow them to earn money today will become a natural part of their lives and remain with them long after the paychecks from you stop.

This following worksheet should be posted where everyone can see it, like on the refrigerator. As a part of their jobs, your kids are responsible for filling this out daily (preferably after each job is completed). You may give them some reminders when you first start the program, but then you should leave it up to them to be responsible for completing it or missing a portion of their pay. No, it is not mean. If you stand by your rules, they won't miss getting paid often. Soon enough you'll find that they've created a great habit.

Paycheck Calculator (Money Mentor)								
Job, Task, or Chore	Saturday	Sunday	Monday	Tuesday	Wednesday	Thursday	Friday	Total
_____								
_____								
_____								
_____								
_____								
_____								

Total Jobs Completed _____
×
Pay Per Successfully Completed Job $_____
=
Total Weekly Paycheck $_____

They will make mistakes—it's not only likely, it's to be expected. When they do, let them experience the consequences. The consequences of our mistakes are how we learn: all successful people have made many mistakes and learned from them. If you always bail your kids out, they won't learn to be responsible adults (and it will be no fault of their own).

Just like with our money, there are rules for how their money is allocated and to be spent. This will involve some oversight on your part. Here is how their overall pay should be allocated.

Business Investments

Yep, that's right—business investments. Just like with the Wealth Builder Lifestyle, your kid's contributions can be dumped in to a growth investment account if you so choose. I on the other hand wanted my kids to learn the art of negotiation, how to evaluate values of different assets, and to have the opportunity to increase the value of their money through compounding means.

If you choose the same they could, for example, run a car wash. Or, they could buy and sell stuff from garage sales, Craigslist, or E-bay. You will have to establish the overall rules for that type of activity, but however you do it you want to make it clear that their money is their working capital to buy materials, products, or advertising. This can be a great hobby as well as a fabulous learning experience. Take a little time to show them how to determine the value of items, what it will cost to market, calculate the expenses of shipping (if applicable), and determine their profit margins (sale price minus total cost of sale).

Growth Investments

This money should be utilized in one of two ways. They can either put it in to a savings account of their own (in which case you would provide a 10% annual return on their money), or (preferably) you could put it in to your online trading account and setup a portfolio of their own so that they can watch their money grow. As they get older, let them research different funds or stocks and move their money around. The main thing is they need to be able to see the value of their investment account because you want them to be totally aware of how money grows.

Personal Expenses

This is the money you would normally spend on them for clothes, school supplies, personal products, and so on. This money should be kept in a savings account or in your possession (until they are old enough to take care of it), but they should be the ones tracking and maintaining the balance. They will take over responsibility for buying their clothes and other necessary items. If they have a phone, for example, you could put the money for it in this category and let them pay it directly. Who knows? Maybe they will want to downgrade to a cheaper plan.

The goal is to connect our children with the value of money while they are still in their peak learning years. Gone will be the days of blowing a fortune on one trendy outfit. That type of money management will force them to have to wear their old clothes every other day of the week.

This plan has had a profound effect on my youngest daughter, who was I guess you could say a little spoiled. As soon as we started following the Money Mentor guidelines, she quickly started evaluating how much she was willing to spend on things like little presents for our dog differently. I remember one day distinctly when I really noticed this in action. She had picked up some $8 toy for the dog and was calculating in her head how much money she would have left if she bought it. Then, she decided it wasn't worth it to her and put it back. That thought process is priceless and has served her very well. She didn't feel sad or pout, she just made a good decision and moved on.

That is a great example of how this system works: she was the one telling herself no—not me—a huge difference! We never have to have conversations about whether or not she can buy things anymore because now it is totally up to her.

CONCLUSION
Fun Money

Last but not least is fun money. You should let them have 100% full control of this money with no restrictions—well, that is, outside of maybe the following one. The rule is that you cannot "eat" your money, which means no buying candy, soda, or other junk food. Outside of that, they can go to the movies, buy toys, whatever they want. They get this money in cold hard cash every Saturday. This works out well because when they don't have the money to go do something with their friends it is all on them. This will encourage them to keep a little stash set aside for those fun times, while building discipline and forming good financial habits. Empowering your kids by putting them in charge of their money is a great opportunity for them to learn. If you follow these rules and don't cave when they come up short, you will be amazed at how well they learn to do on their own.

Income Allocations

How you choose to allocate the percentage of their total pay that goes towards each category is up to you. You need to decide what works and will fit your goals. What I chose to do was set aside 25% for fun money, 40% for personal expenses, 20% for growth investments, and 15% for business investments.

If they miss their income-earning opportunities, make sure they still stick to the allocated percentages strictly—no robbing Peter to pay Paul! If they have to go a month without having a phone, so be it. Letting them change their allocations would just teach them that they don't have to have good financial habits and can get the reward without the responsibility of performing.

Paycheck Distribution Calculator

Here is a tool you can use to easily calculate their weekly paycheck allocations. I would advise that you let them start calculating their own paychecks and allocations as soon as they are capable of it because it will help build their money calculating skills.

Paycheck Distribution (Money Mentor)			
Pay Allocations	Total Weekly Pay Earned	Percentage of Pay	Category Total
Business Investments	$_____	× ____% =	$_____
Growth Investments		× ____% =	$_____
Personal Money		× ____% =	$_____
Fun Money		× ____% =	$_____

Just like adults, they need to be aware of and track their results so they can see the effects of their actions. To achieve this, they need to be aware of their total net worth. For my kids this was a big deal because as their net worth grew they developed a sense of pride about what they were accomplishing. This became a topic that they were all too happy to talk about, which resulted in them getting a lot of positive feedback.

Setup a time once a month to check their accounts and update the following net worth statement. It is good to do this monthly with kids as their attention spans are so short. The frequent revisits will help keep them focused through repetition. Let them do as much of this as they can on their own as soon as possible.

NOTES :

_____

_____

_____

CONCLUSION

Net Worth Evaluator (Money Mentor) Date ___/___/_____			
Asset	**Value**	**Liability**	**Value**
Business Investments	$_____	Loans	$_____
Growth Investments	$_____	Other Debts	$_____
Personal Money	$_____	**Total Liabilities**	$_____
Fun Money	$_____		
Other Cash	$_____		
Personal Property		**Net Worth**	
_____	$_____	Total Assets	$_____
_____	$_____	Total Liabilities	$_____
_____	$_____	**Total Net Worth**	$_____
_____	$_____	(net worth = assets – liabilities)	
_____	$_____	*"You can choose to live the habits of the lifestyles of the rich and famous or the habits of the poor and destitute. You decide!"*	
Total Assets	$_____		

Here is one more form that you may want to use to track their monthly income. It can be a good historical reference so they can see their track record over time.

Monthly Income (Money Mentor)	
Month _____ Year _____	Weekly Income
Week One	$_____
Week Two	$_____
Week Three	$_____
Week Four	$_____
Week Five	$_____
Total Monthly Income	$_____

You may want to get a three ring binder or other folder that they can use to keep their records in. This way they can look back over the years and see how they amassed so much wealth. If you start them on this program early, by the time they are ready to buy a car they will be able to purchase it with their own money. They will also have a sense of pride that is unimaginable and take much better care of it than they would if you had bought it for them.

If you choose to try this simple system with your kids, I think you will be amazed with the results, just like I was. Sure, it will be a little bit of work, but I promise you it will be well worth it in the end. Oddly enough, teaching is one of the best ways to learn, so while you are teaching them you will also be sharpening your own skills. This will also be a great bonding experience and let's face it: what loving parent wouldn't want a great bonding experience?

NOTES :

_____

_____

_____

_____

_____

_____

_____

_____

_____

_____

CLOSING THOUGHTS

Without a doubt, living a Wealth Builder Lifestyle will empower you to consistently create wealth. How successful you are in the transition from where you are to a true wealth builder will be dictated by your dedication to mastering your personal finances.

If there is one thing you take away from this, I hope you learn *how* to think about money, not *what* to think. This program has a pretty formal outline of how to manage your finances to build wealth, however, there is no exact strategy that will fit everyone and be the most effective approach to achieve their goals.

This program is filled with time-tested principles that work. How you can best use them to the fullest extent comes down to your ability to think through your application and exact strategy.

We all have the God-given ability to become good thinkers. Your ability to think intelligently is not predetermined. By working through this program, you have taken a huge step towards strengthening your financial skills and decision-making abilities. This should not be the end, just part of your continuous journey in improving your knowledge. The one sure thing is that wealth and success will always follow the informed thinkers.

We live in a world that is changing faster than any time in history. Today's rapid pace will affect your wealth strategy, lifestyle, and almost every aspect of your life. I continually focus on learning the latest strategies of what works in all aspects of life and I encourage you to do the same. Setup a plan for constant improvement and you will always thrive and prosper to the best of your abilities.

The world will give you what you deserve, so make the most of your abilities and leave the struggling to the lazy and slothful.

For electronic copies of the worksheets in this book, please go to www.WealthBuilderLifestyle.com/tools.

ABOUT THE AUTHOR

Daniel Hartjoy is the founder of Methods For Mastery, Inc. and the author of multiple books dedicated to helping people break through their personal barriers and achieve their ultimate dreams. He is well known for his commitment to helping others reach their highest levels of performance and personal success. His ability to see the best in every person and situation is legendary. Through the use of a philanthropist approach to sharing his abundance of life changing strategies, he is dedicated to impacting a much broader spectrum of humanity. One of his primary objectives is to reach out to those who typically fall through the cracks and get left behind.

Having come from humble beginnings with no college education, he has used his unique approaches to take his income from $8 an hour, to earning over $100,000 in a single month. He has worked his way up through the corporate world smashing through boundaries his education and background said he couldn't cross. He has also started multiple companies and broke and rewrote the rules that businesses are supposed to operate under, leading to phenomenal growth in record time. This includes launching an out of state company he would manage remotely that would go from nothing to almost $3,000,000 in revenue the first year, with a profit margin in excess of 30%. It was through these experiences he realized that life has so much more to offer us than what we ask of it. If someone can break free of their false beliefs of what they expect from and hope to achieve in life, their world can be changed forever. Through the use of his books, live events and personal coaching he continues to make his life changing message and strategies available around the globe.

COMING SOON
December - 2014

The

WEALTH BUILDER
Lifestyle 2.0

The Millionaire Blueprint

In this highly anticipated follow up to The Wealth Builder Lifestyle: How The Other 99% Can Get Rich book, you'll learn to create your own personalized Millionaire Blueprint. This will be your wealth creation action plan from now until you retire. Not only will you create a detailed plan of action but the wealth forcaster will allow you to see just how much wealth you can expect to obtain during your lifetime if you follow your blueprint.

Gone will be the days of working a lifetime only to find out you came up short of your retirement financial needs. If your blueprint doesn't have the potential to reach your goals, change it now!

Don't take Daniel Hartjoy's claim "anyone can retire a millionaire regardless of their income" on his word, let him show you how it's possible in black and white detail.

Included he will also share his investing 202 strategies for rapidly creating more wealth. By now you should know these will not be get rich quick schemes but genuine and powerful wealth building techniques.

---

www.ingramcontent.com/pod-product-compliance
Lightning Source LLC
Chambersburg PA
CBHW021044090426
42738CB00006B/176